BY THE AUTO EDITORS OF
CONSUMER GUIDE®

ELITE CARS

BEEKMAN HOUSE
New York

CONTENTS

This edition published by
Beekman House,
distributed by
Crown Publishers, Inc.
225 Park Avenue South
New York, New York 10003

ISBN: 0-517-63898-3

Manufactured in Yugoslavia by CGP Delo
h g f e d c b a

CREDITS

Photography and illustrations were furnished in cooperation with the following. **Ferrari GTO:** Joe Oliver; Fredi Valentini, Industrie Pininfarina S.p.A.; Andre Van De Putte. **Vector W2 TwinTurbo:** Vehicle Design Force. **Ford RS 200:** Ford Motor Company. **Ferrari Testarossa:** Mr. De Franchi of Ferrari; Industrie Pininfarina S.p.A.; Frank E. Peiler; David Tellefsen. **Buick Wildcat:** Floyd C. Joliet, General Motors Design; Tom Pond, Buick Motor Division, General Motors Corporation. **Corvette Roadster:** Ed Lechtzin, Chevrolet Motor Division, General Motors; Roland Flessner; Richard D. Hawthorne. **De Tomaso Pantera GT5:** David Gooley; Stauffer Classics, Ltd.; Xaver Jehle Industrie. **Porsche 959:** Begona Gosch and Klaus Parr, Dr. Ing. h.c.F. Porsche A.G.

INTRODUCTION

There's very little you need to know as you dive into this book. The title says it all.

So do the cars. Of course, they're all very expensive. Even the cheapest, the Corvette roadster, will set you back 35 big ones, while the Porsche 959 is so exotic as to be unobtainable by anyone not affiliated with Weissach's rally team. And the experimental Buick Wildcat isn't for sale at *any* price, though your local dealer may have something very much like it in not too many years.

Naturally, they're also very fast, far beyond the abilities of mortal machines. In this league, 120 mph is merely an *entry-level* maximum speed.

But it scarcely matters that you can't legally drive any of them in this country at even half that velocity, because they're exciting to look at. Except for the 'Vette and Porsche 959, all employ the mid-engine layout once reserved for racing, and thus end up being purposeful rather than pretty. Some are aggressively serious (De Tomaso Pantera GT5, Ferrari Testarossa), others sleek and sensual (Vector W2 TwinTurbo, Ferrari GTO). The Ford RS 200 rally car? Let's call it "distinctive."

But most of all, these are no-compromise cars designed for the ultimate in driving satisfaction—and sometimes, skill. That's what makes them *high-performance* elite cars. And well worth reading about. Enjoy!

Flat-12 engine and Pininfarina bodywork mark Ferrari's line-topping Testarossa.

FERRARI
GTO

The GTO of the early Sixties is one of the most valued Ferraris. Despite today's stricter safety and emissions regulations, the new GTO handily exceeds the original in performance.

At first glance, the Ferrari GTO is reminiscent of the 308 GTB. Only 200 GTOs are being built.

Once again, Ferrari recalls a heralded name from the past to adorn its latest race-bred road rocket. Lest one think that the company in Maranello lacks imagination when developing monikers, consider that Ferrari has a proud heritage and that the original GTO of the early Sixties is one of the most valued Ferraris of all time. Introduced in February of 1962, the first GTO was a dual-purpose street and racing machine that sported a sleek, rounded coupe body and an engine similar to that of the Ferrari Testa Rossa race car of the late Fifties. The 3.0-liter single-overhead-cam V-12 had two-valve heads, six twin-choke Webers, and an output purported to be near 300 brake horsepower. Formidable contenders in the GT class at such races as Sebring and Le Mans, the front-engine GTOs racked up an impressive string of victories, many of which were recorded long after production ceased in 1964.

Ferrari's marketing wisdom in reviving the famous GTO emblem may be questioned, but their engineering prowess cannot—the new model continues the GTO legacy. Despite the stricter safety and emissions regulations with which today's automobiles are forced to comply, the new GTO handily exceeds the performance figures of the original. In fact, the latest thoroughbred from the Ferrari stables promises to be the fastest street car ever to bear the symbol of the prancing horse.

As if to uphold tradition while taking advantage of recent technological developments, the GTO is a curious combination of old and new. The voluptuous curves of the body will remind aficionados of the 308 GTB that has been produced for 10 years now, although many of the 308's dimensions seem to have been altered in order to accommodate the GTO's north-south engine placement and broader stance. The neophyte would be hard-pressed to distinguish the new Pininfarina design from the old. Park the two vehicles side by side, however, and the differences become more apparent. The GTO sports a deeper chin spoiler underlining a grille housing quadruple rectangular driving lamps. It also has a much more aggressive stance due to the four-inch-wider track and consequently wider front fenders. At the rear of the car, the GTO has two additional ducts on

each side of the body, one beneath the door on the rocker panel and the other between the rear side window and the rear roof pillar. Like those at the front, the rear fenders are more bulbous due to the increased tread width, and three vertical slots were added behind the drive wheels. Finally, the rear overhang

is somewhat less, while the rear spoiler is more pronounced. In short, the GTO looks like a hot-rod version of the GTB. If you liked the GTB, chances are very good that you'll like the GTO.

Yet, while the GTB may have an appearance similar to that of the GTO, its structural composition is entirely differ-

ent. Covering the steel-tube frame is a body comprised of various space-age composites utilizing Kevlar, fiberglass, carbon fiber, and plastic. The resulting structure is so strong and light that despite the additional weight of the turbochargers, intercoolers, and a second gas tank, the GTO actually weighs about 250 pounds less than the 308, and the GTO is lighter than its new sistership—the Testarossa—by more than 750 pounds.

The arrangement of the cockpit again is patterned after the 308. Pleated leather seats with ample side bolstering hold you in place as you grip the flat,

Opposite page, top: The rear emblems. Bottom: Front view, with deep spoiler. Top: The GTO's vents and scoops along the side. Above, left: The GTO's engine hatch. Above, right: The leather seats are ready for driver and passenger.

three-spoke, leather-covered steering wheel. The instrument panel holds orange-on-black gauges, and protruding from the center console is the traditionally tall, spindly shift lever guided by a chromeplated gate. New, however, is the pseudo suede covering the dashboard in place of the usual leather.

The GTO's powerplant breaks some new ground for Ferrari. The exotic, aluminum V-8 is basically similar to the engine that is used in the 308, but with lower compression and a one-millimeter decrease in bore size. The resulting displacement for the V-8 is 2.8 liters, or just over half that of the 4942cc 12-cylinder Testarossa. An integrated electronic ignition and fuel-injection system by Weber-Marelli is at the heart of the new engine, but twin IHI turbochargers each forcing compressed air through separate Behr intercoolers provide the soul. The turbo system is the first forced-air induction system to be utilized

by a Ferrari street car. Along with the now-common four-valve heads, the engine's combination of technology is good for 394 bhp at 7000 rpm and 366 lbs/ft of torque at 3800 rpm. Both of the figures are higher than the respective numbers for the 5.0-liter, normally aspirated Testarossa engine, and they add a good 50 percent to the 308's statistics. Take into account the GTO's substantially lighter weight—then the factory's claims that the 0-60 sprint takes less than 4.9 seconds, that a quarter-mile can be covered in 12.7 seconds, and that top speed hovers around 189.5 miles per hour become extremely plausible. While the figures on GTOs modified for the United States may suffer somewhat in maximum velocity because of meeting emission standards, initial reports indicate that very little acceleration capability is lost.

Some of the Ferrari's exotic contemporaries are like high-strung racehorses

The GTO is everything the 308 has been, and more—more power, more performance, and, of course, more money. A price tag of approximately $125,000 will limit ownership.

—great in a flat-out sprint, but hardly the mount of choice for an everyday crawl through traffic. Though sentencing the GTO to the doldrums of a daily commute may seem an injustice, the car would be perfectly tractable in performing such a task. If you can restrain yourself, the GTO can putter around town with the best of them, while still leaving you secure in the knowledge that a herd of horses is ready to stampede should patience wear thin. Mashing the throttle at low engine speeds produces dreaded turbo lag, but doing so is akin to lighting the fuse on a stick of dynamite. The reaction may not be immediate, but the engine explodes with a frenzied burst of power as the boost comes up. The explosion is as if the soup-can-size pistons had suddenly become 55-gallon drums.

The GTO is everything the 308 has been, and more—more power, more performance, and, of course, more money. With a price tag of approximately $125,000, ownership of the super auto will be possible only for a few. The factory has never produced automobiles in anything approaching large numbers, and if Ferrari maintains its original projection of 200 total units to qualify the model for Group B racing, the GTOs promise to be as scarce and highly prized as are their namesakes, of which only 39 units were made. Due to the exclusivity and the extraordinary performance of the new GTO, it seems destined to join the older model as one of the most revered models ever to bear the Ferrari marque.

MAJOR SPECIFICATIONS

Ferrari GTO

General: Mid-engine, rear-drive, two-passenger coupe; steel-tube frame, body of Kevlar, fiberglass, carbon fiber, and plastic. **Base price:** Approx. $125,000. Ferrari S.p.A., Modena, Italy.

Dimensions and Capacities

Wheelbase (in.):	96.5
Overall length (in.):	168.9
Overall width (in.):	75.2
Overall height (in.):	44.1
Track front (in.):	61.4
Track rear (in.):	61.5
Curb weight (lbs):	2557 (factory)
Fuel tank (gal):	31.7

Drivetrain

Engine type:	Aluminum, 90° V-8
Displacement (cc/ci):	2855/174
Compression ratio:	7.6:1
Fuel delivery:	

Weber-Marelli electronic ignition and fuel injection, twin IHI turbochargers, two Behr intercoolers

Net bhp @ rpm:	394 @ 7000
Net lbs/ft torque @ rpm:	366 @ 3800
Transmission type:	Five-speed manual
Final drive ratio:	2.90:1

Chassis

Front suspension:
Independent, unequal-length control arms, Koni coil-over shocks, sway bars

Rear suspension:
Independent, unequal-length control arms, Koni coil-over shocks, sway bars

Steering:	Rack-and-pinion
Turns lock-to-lock:	2.8
Turn diameter (ft):	39.4

Brake system:
12.2" vented discs, front and rear

Wheels:
Three-piece aluminum; 8" × 16" front, 10" × 16" rear

Tires:
Goodyear NCT; 225/50VR-16 front, 255/50VR-16 rear

Performance

0-62.1 mph (sec):	4.9 (factory)
0-¼-mi. (sec):	12.7 (factory)
Top speed (mph):	189.5 (factory)

Opposite page, top: While tractable at normal speeds, the GTO's 394 brake horsepower is at the driver's beck and call. **Lower left:** Ferrari's symbol appears on the front fender, behind the wheel. **Lower right:** The headlights swivel out of the front hood. **Above:** The beautifully styled Ferrari GTO has a top speed claimed by the factory to be 189.5 miles per hour.

VECTOR W2 TWINTURBO

The Vector gives *quantity* and *direction* concrete form as applied to automobiles. It's an all-American car that employs space-age technology.

Vector is a term that you might remember from physics class—a quantity that has magnitude and direction is a vector. Vectors are represented by arrows, and computation of the resultant magnitude and direction of any number of vectors that originate from a given point is possible. Quantity and direction—apply these two concepts to the automobile world and you won't be surprised by the Vector W2 TwinTurbo. That is, you won't be sur-

While the Vector W2 TwinTurbo benefits from the application of space-age materials, some elements have been proven over time.

prised if you take your applications to the extreme. The concept of quantity leads to visions of unlimited horsepower and torque, of inordinate muscle that can be applied in any direction by way of a light, nimble chassis. The TwinTurbo embodies it all, but the car is more. Other adjectives must be applied—*breathtaking, wind-cheating, brutal, high-tech, aerodynamic, state-of-the-art, futuristic, savage, American*. Most of these adjectives apply to the Vector as they do to few other cars.

The Vector is, after all is said and done, an automobile. Although unlike others in so many ways, it still has wheels, a body, a chassis, an engine, and running gear. It isn't a spacecraft, although it will remind you of one... and for good reason. Vector designer Gerald A. Wiegert applied contemporary aerospace engineering techniques and processes to every inch and every aspect of the Vector from its very beginning. The result is a visually astounding car that boasts top speeds in excess of 200 mph, 0-60 times at 4.0 seconds and under, an 11-second quarter-mile, and 1.0-G lateral acceleration on the skid pad. The 2500-pound body

carries an engine capable of developing well over 600 bhp, even twice that much. With such power potential, all aspects of the Vector *have* to be right.

Jerry Wiegert started the Vector project in the early Seventies, and he is responsible for the design, execution, and engineering layout of the car. Through his Vehicle Design Force, a consulting company that he founded in 1972, the Vector Cars division has emerged as only one of a number of directions taken by the company, including the development of alternate energy-type vehicles. The underlying philosophy behind Vector Cars is that an exotic American automobile should blend aerospace technology, materials, and construction techniques with an aerodynamic design in a no-holds-barred manner. The automobile should be durable, reliable, easily maintained and repaired, comfortable, and safe. Uncompromising aerospace construction and design techniques applied to the normal facets of the automobile have yielded the Vector W2 Twin-Turbo, unique and unparalleled in automotive history, at least in the company's mind. Its judgment may

well be correct. The company calls the Vector a High Technology Multi-Role Exotic (HTME).

The 42.5-inch-high body has a wedge shape, low in the front and angled to use the wind's downforce to advantage. Other aerodynamic applications are the double-element rear wing, the smooth underside, and the flush-mounted windows and door handles. The upper and lower parts of the body are integrated, yielding greater strength and improved drag considerations. The body's skin is a composite of materials—Kevlar fabric, graphite, and glass fibers bonded by epoxy resin. It is strong, light in weight, dent-proof, and corrosion-free. The body is styled with a line from front to rear, along each side, that suggests the car's name—Vector. The line implies direction and, along with the visual impact of the car, staggering magnitude. The radical slope of the windshield and dramatic impression of the body's wedge shape in general only attest to the functionalism of the total package. The two doors elevate, but not like the gullwings of the 300SL Mercedes or the more recent Bricklin. They might remind you of the

Lamborghini Countach, for they tip up and forward in a similar manner.

Once the doors have been opened, the interior is easily accessible. At first glance, it looks almost spartan. The dashboard is plain, and the only dial-like circular shapes in the interior are found on the doors. Looking like holes cut into a metal bulkhead to lighten it, they are the speakers of a sound system. Recaro bucket seats invite the driver and passenger to settle in and enjoy. The seats are infinitely adjustable, of course, and electrically heated. The aircraft-type five-point seat restraints promise secure protection. The cockpit offers so much room that an optional three-place seat may be ordered. With no center console, there is plenty of room for the occupants.

Opposite page: The 42.5-inch-high body has skin that is a composite of Kevlar fabric, graphite, and glass fibers bonded by epoxy resin. Above: The engine is mounted transversely ahead of the rear wheels. The body also has a double-element wing, a smooth underside, and flush-mounted outer windows and trim. Right: The doors tilt forward to allow relatively easy access.

The automatic gearshift selector is flush-mounted in an indentation found in the bulkhead to the left of the driver.

Instrumentation is in the form of a "heads-up display," which reflects primary information from the speedometer and tachometer onto the windshield so that the driver's eyes need not leave the road in order to read them. The heads-up display is common in advanced military fighter planes, such as the F-16. Other instruments are in the form of bar graphs, stacked horizontally and lighted so that when any one of the 10 bars breaks a vertical plane, it attracts attention, thereby affording constant vigilance of the engine's functions.

Wiegert considers the engine that was chosen for the Vector to be an excellent combination of durability, performance, and efficiency. It's an aluminum-block 350-cid Chevrolet V-8, the short-block Donovan engine that was developed and engineered specifically for racing. The 350 has survived more than 25 years because of its dependability. In the Donovan form, it weighs half of what an iron-block engine would weigh, and it benefits from having heat-treated aluminum parts available for the precision required by the Vector. The blueprinted block is only part of the whole engine's story. Because of the wide range of racing applications for the Donovan through the years, many configurations have been tested, allowing Vector Cars to custom fit the engine to the particular needs of an individual customer. Vector's engineers have fitted their "typical" engine with twin turbochargers and fuel injection, allowing a range in horsepower rating from 600 to 1300, depending on the customer's desires. In its 600 bhp trim, the Donovan meets the strictest state and federal emissions regulations. While the Donovan V-8 is one of the most powerful, it is also one of the easiest engines in its class to maintain and in which to replace components. It sits transversely behind the passenger compartment, where it feeds its power to the rear wheels through a General Motors Turbo 425 Hydra-Matic transmission, the transmission that has been thoroughly tested over the last few years in the Eldorado/Toronado series and in the GMC motor homes. The 425 Hydra-Matic may be used either as a manual (sans clutch) or automatic, driving the wheels through a no-slip, dual-drive differential.

The drivetrain is conceived in modular form for ease of service access. There are three distinct modules—one each for engine, transmission, and the differential/final drive. Any one or combination of the three modules may be dropped quickly for service or changing. Within each module certain parts are replaceable without the removal of any other parts: engine module—fuel distributor, fuel injectors, fuel pump, alternator, water pump, oil pump, turbochargers, wastegates, power steering pump, and air conditioning compressor; transmission module—chain and sprockets, valve body, governor, and modulator; differential/final drive—input gear, output gear, and stub axles.

The Vector's chassis is as innovative as the drivetrain, using aerospace processes and materials for strength and rigidity. The chassis weighs a mere 350 pounds and is constructed of high-stress aluminum alloy skins joined by epoxy and stainless-steel rivets to form

the monocoque, which integrates a structural steel alloy roll cage that is reinforced with an aluminum honeycomb panel. The suspension is fabricated from a lightweight steel alloy. It has unequal-length A-arms in front and trailing arms with a de Dion tube in the rear. All shock-absorbing units have adjustable damping, rebound, and spring preload, which makes it possible for the driver to dial in the suspension that yields his own ride preferences.

Opposite page: The Chevrolet Donovan aluminum short-block engine has been proven in race cars of all types. Top: The Vector's skin fits over a chassis (above) that incorporates a roll bar. The chassis weighs only 350 pounds, due to the use of aerospace processes and materials such as aluminum, stainless steel, and epoxy.

MAJOR SPECIFICATIONS
Vector W2 TwinTurbo

General: Transverse mid-engine, rear-drive, two-seat coupe. Semi-monocoque and composite structure chassis with composite body. **Base price:** $150,000. Vector Cars, Venice, CA.

Dimensions and Capacities

Wheelbase (in.):	na
Overall length (in.):	172.0
Overall width (in.):	76.0
Overall height (in.):	42.5
Track front (in.):	63.0
Track rear (in.):	65.0
Curb weight (lbs.):	
2700, 43%/57% front/rear weight distribution	
Fuel tank (gal.):	30.0

Drivetrain

Engine type:	
Chevrolet Donovan aluminum block	
Displacement (cc/ci):	5737/350
Compression ratio:	7.0:1
Fuel delivery:	
Twin-turbocharged, fuel-injected	
Net bhp @ rpm:	600 (+) @ 6000
Net lbs/ft torque @ rpm:	na
Transmission type:	
Three-speed automatic, selectable fully manual or automatic control	
Final drive ratio:	2.42:1

Chassis

Front suspension:
Unequal-length A-arms with concentric coil springs and shocks
Rear suspension:
De Dion tube with upper and lower trailing arms, diagonal lateral stabilizer and coil springs and shocks
Steering:
Variable ratio, rack-and-pinion, tilt telescoping wheel

Turns lock-to-lock:	3.25
Turn diameter (ft.):	na
Brake system:	
Four-wheel, four-piston caliper discs	
Wheels:	

Three-piece design—9″ × 15″ front, 12″ × 15″ rear

Tires:	50-series, VR-rated radials

Performance

0-60 mph (sec.):	3.9
0-¼-mi. (sec.):	11.0
mph @ ¼-mi.:	na
Speeds in gears:	na
Top speed (mph):	240 +
EPA city mpg:	na
EPA highway mpg:	na

The Vector represents extremely well-planned and highly developed automotive engineering of a type that few will have the pleasure to experience or even study from proximity. Projected annual output is 50 to 70.

The chore of halting the forward motion of the TwinTurbo falls to the Lockheed competition racing brakes. Four-wheel ventilated discs and aluminum four-piston calipers serve the high-speed Vector's need to stop as dramatically as it accelerates. The wheels are of a three-piece modular design, cold-forged for greater strength, and they carry 225/50VR-15 tires in front and 285/50VR-15s in the rear.

A number of intriguing safety features have been built into the Vector. The full steel roll cage is capable of protecting passengers at speeds well above legal limits. With knowledge born of aircraft and formula racing body construction, the Vector is built with three stages of crash protection. The first stage of protection is from the elastic, resilient bumpers. The second is from the energy-absorbing bumper mounts —hydraulic shock absorbers. The third stage has to do with the chassis construction itself, with it being designed to deform in its extremities up to the passenger cage. The deformation gives way to impact, helping to absorb the shock of a collision rather than passing it on to the occupants within the roll cage. Another safety consideration is the location and construction of the fuel cell. It is also within the confines of the roll cage, and it is made of explosion-suppressing foam, a bladder-like affair that was initially designed for use in aircraft. To help reduce the possibility of fire, stainless-steel braided fuel lines are used. Automatic and manual fire extinguishing systems are also built into the car. The electrical system is protected by aircraft-type breakers, which warn of an overload with sound and visual signals.

With attention given to safety, and with at least 600 horsepower available to the driver, this exotic super automobile seems an unlikely candidate to be touted as an efficient machine in the bargain. Yet that's what is claimed with regard to mileage figures when the car is driven within legal speed limits. The Vector achieves about 20 miles per gallon under normal driving conditions and offers good low-speed tractability. It is as easily handled at low speeds as at high. The Vector W2 TwinTurbo represents extremely well-planned and highly developed automotive engineering of a type that few will ever have the pleasure to experience or even to study from proximity. With projected output of Vectors at 50 to 70 units per year and a sticker price of $150,000 and more, it is truly a super automobile of exotic proportions.

Above: The Vector has more than ample interior room—up to three people fit widthwise. Left: The Vector has elements born of aircraft and spacecraft engineering, in materials and safety considerations. Opposite page, top: Not only are the lines of the Vector at one with flying machines, so are important aspects of its aerodynamic design. Bottom: Truly an exotic super automobile, the Vector is well-conceived in every detail.

FORD RS 200

Ford's division of European Motorsports built an all-out rally car from the ground up. Some of racing's most talented people contributed to the process of building this supercar.

In competition form, the RS 200 will speed across every type of terrain, its scoops, vents, and dams directing air where needed.

Another Ford supercar is being built, and it promises to have the impact of the GT-40s of the past and the more recent GTP Mustangs. The only difference is that a street version will be available to the enthusiast who can afford one. The Ford RS 200 goes beyond yesterday's Ford Shelby Mustangs and even today's SVO Mustangs. Ford of Europe is undertaking the development program of the RS 200, a turbocharged, two-seat, two-/four-wheel-drive sports car intended for FIA Group B road rallying. The RS 200 is designed and built from the ground up, employing the most recent technology for the highly competitive works cars and for those to be sold to outside rally customers. At least 200 units for the street must be manufactured for FIA homologation.

The advantage of building an automobile from scratch, free of production car restraints, is that the designers and engineers set their own parameters based on the car's ultimate application. Ford's division of European Motorsports, directed by Stuart Turner, set the objectives for the RS 200: Build a two-seat sports car that can compete as a rally-winner against the likes of Peugeot, Porsche, Lancia, and Audi, and can double as a special road machine in civilian dress. The development program, begun in 1983, had to produce a "no compromise" design relative to power output, drivetrain, and chassis. Turner initiated the project with a clean slate, and applied the resources of some of the best engineering talent in the world. Body styling was by Filippo Sapino of Ford's Ghia Design Studio in Turin, Italy, and by Ford's British and German European design groups. Mechanical design/development was by Ford Motorsports chief engineer John Wheeler, in consultation with Formula 1 Grand Prix designer Tony Southgate. The project filled the clean slate with a remarkable rally car—a supercar. The Ford RS 200 has a mid-engine, front-mounted transaxle layout, a 50/50 weight distribution, and a driver-selectable rear-/four-wheel-drive system.

The Ford 1.8-liter four-cylinder engine has four valves per cylinder, double overhead camshaft, fuel injection, and Garrett AiResearch air-to-air intercooled turbocharger. The preproduction model develops more than 230 brake horsepower. Competition engines

The development program for the RS 200 began in 1983. The end result of the program was to be a "no compromise" design relative to power output, drivetrain, and chassis.

probably will reach 380 bhp. The engine is placed behind the driver longitudinally, ahead of the rear axle, from which a short drive shaft connects to a front-mounted transaxle. Another drive shaft runs from the transaxle back to the rear wheels. The rear wheels are always driven; the engagement of the front wheels is optional. The driver can choose the configuration needed and even adjust the degree of torque to be sent to the front wheels in a four-wheel-drive situation. It's possible to designate no torque to the front, 37 percent to the front, or 50 percent. When the driver encounters dry pavement conditions, the powertrain works most efficiently in rear-wheel drive only. Optimum balance for almost all other conditions is through the 37/63 torque split. Under very slippery water and ice conditions, the car has its best traction with a 50/50 split. The choice can be made under power as conditions dictate, even in the middle of a curve. Shift control through the five-speed transmission is precise because the gearbox, located immediately behind the front axle, is part of the transaxle.

Made from a combination of materials for strength and durability, the high-tech chassis employs aluminum, steel, carbon, and plastic reinforced with aramid fiber. Tony Southgate master-minded the development of the chassis, bringing Formula 1 Grand Prix design experience to bear. The floor section, sills, and bulkheads begin as

an aluminum honeycomb sandwich sheet, under which a protective steel stone-and-impact shield is bonded and riveted. The extremely strong and light central tunnel is constructed of molded carbon and aramid-fiber reinforced plastic. Steel extensions, bonded and riveted to the front and rear bulkheads, carry the front transaxle, engine mounts, and rear drive unit. The layout of the engine, running gear, and suspension relative to the chassis reflects singleness of purpose—accessibility. Rallying typically requires immediate, complete changes or welding of running gear and suspension components. Ford's goal for the time needed to change transmissions was under 10 minutes, made possible by placing the driveline components along the central tunnel so that everything is easily reached from underneath. Aerospace and Formula 1 construction techniques made the chassis even stronger via integration with parts of the upper body. The roof and upper door openings are constructed of the reinforced plastic found in the chassis, and the upper body incorporates a tubular roll bar. The stressed chassis and body are bolted together to form a unit

unusually high in strength for its light weight (estimated curb weight is 2315 pounds). An adjustable suspension of lightweight aluminum has a double-wishbone configuration front and rear. The running gear may be adjusted to meet the driver's needs, with chassis mounts for two ground-clearance settings—one for smooth roads and one for rough roads.

Ghia's Filippo Sapino included as many Ford Sierra parts and design details as he could, while attempting to develop the most competitive rally body possible for Ford. The Sierra's windshield and modified doors were used, for instance, to hold down replacement costs. Rally considerations dictated the form of much of Sapino's body design—the wedge shape, the minimum-clearance front and rear overhangs, the flared fenders capable of wide rubber, the wraparound air dam, the front-end openings for fog/driving lights, and the integrated spoiler across the back. Scoops and ducts poke from the body's surface, with an exhaust duct on the forward part of the hood for the air that has cooled the radiators, and a full-width intake scoop along the rear of the

Above: Testing the RS 200, the developers have found ways to improve its handling and aerodynamics. Opposite page: The homologation version of the car will offer at least 200 enthusiasts the opportunity to have a taste of the supercar's rallying qualities.

roofline to direct air through the air-to-air turbo intercooler. The RS 200's interior is intended to provide a workable space with complete instrumentation giving information to the driver. Modifications on the body were made after wind-tunnel testing, and detail work to enable easy access to the engine compartment was accomplished through work with Pilbeam Racing Enterprises.

High-tech construction techniques and engineering, along with rally-based styling, have given Ford a super-car with 0-60 times of less than five seconds and a chassis and drivetrain capable of handling any road surface. An estimated $40,000 price tag will probably deliver the road version. The prototypes have been tested, with the help of three-time World Champion Formula 1 driver Jackie Stewart and a number of international rally drivers, and reworked to gain a competitive edge. The Ford team will be ready to field the race version of the car by the end of the 1985 international season.

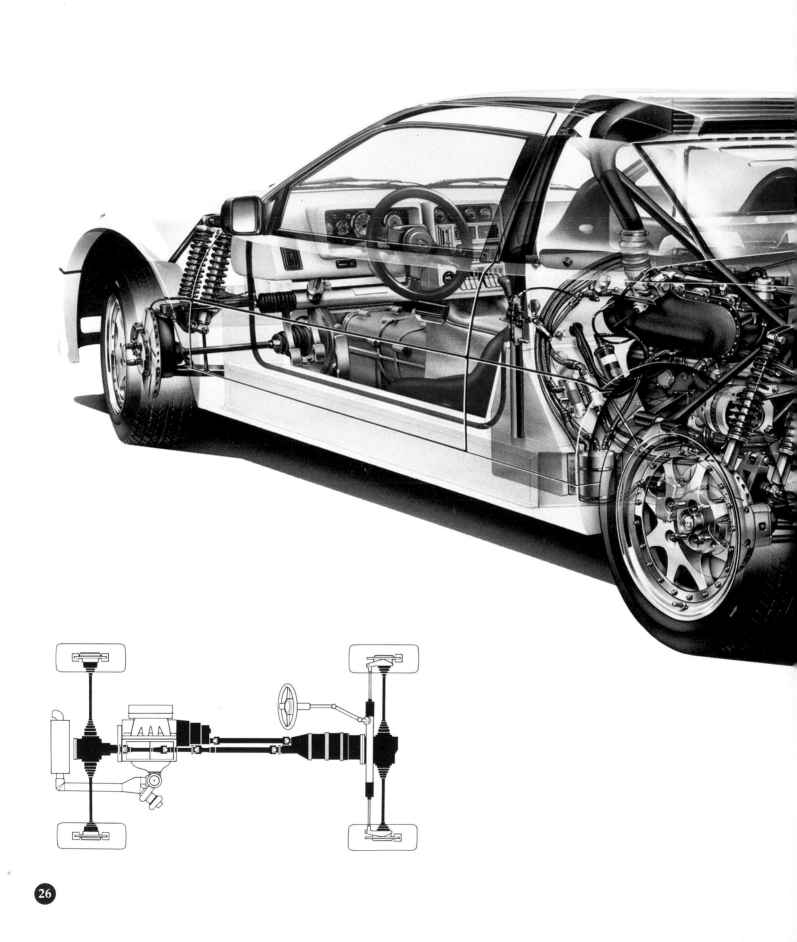

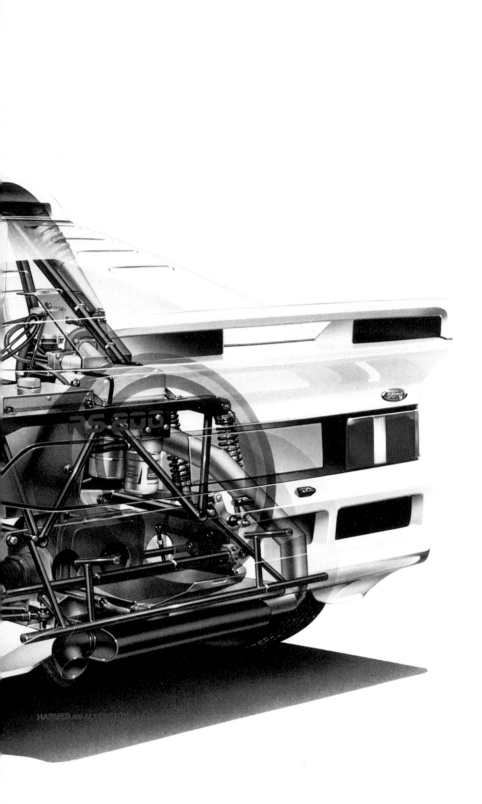

Above: The cutaway reveals the integrated roll bar, the dual shocks per wheel, the heat escape slots in the rear window, the positioning of the "spare" tire, the purpose of the roof air scoop. Left: The layout of the RS 200's drivetrain shows the drive shaft running from the longitudinally positioned engine to the front transaxle, then another shaft running from the front to the rear axle. The rear wheels are constantly driven, and the driver has the option of engaging the front wheels.

MAJOR SPECIFICATIONS
Ford RS 200

General: Mid-engine, rear-drive or variable four-wheel drive, two-seat coupe. Composite monocoque, aluminum honeycomb, mild steel, carbon fiber and aramid fiber reinforced resin, bonded, riveted, and bolted; high-grade steel tubular roll cage. **Price:** est. $40,000. Ford of Europe.

Dimensions and Capacities

Wheelbase (in.):	99.6
Overall length (in.):	157.5
Overall width (in.):	69.0
Overall height (in.):	na
Track front (in.):	59.1
Track rear (in.):	58.9
Curb weight (lbs.):	2315
Fuel tank (gal.):	30.6

Drivetrain

Engine type:
Ford BDT 16-valve twin-cam four-cylinder turbo

Displacement (cc/ci):	1800/109.8
Compression ratio:	8.2:1

Fuel delivery:
Garrett AiResearch T.03/04 air-to-air intercooled turbocharger, Ford electronic injection with EEC IV controls.

Net bhp @ rpm (DIN):	230 @ 6000 rpm
Net lbs/ft torque @ rpm (DIN):	280 @ 4500 rpm
Transmission type:	five-speed manual
Final drive ratio:	4.375:1

Chassis

Front suspension:
Double wishbone, twin coil spring and damper units, anti-roll bar, alternative ride height settings

Rear suspension:
Double wishbone, twin coil spring and damper units, anti-roll bar, adjustable toe control link, alternative ride height settings

Steering:	rack-and-pinion
Turns lock-to-lock:	2.3
Turn diameter (ft.):	31.5

Brake system:
11.4-in. ventilated discs front and rear

Wheels:
Speedline composite alloy 16 × 8-in.

Tires: 225/50VR-16 Pirelli P700 radial

Performance

0-60 mph (sec.):	under 5.0
0-¼-mi. (sec.):	na
mph @ ¼-mi.:	na
Speeds in gears:	I—42.7
	II—62.9
	III—87.1
	IV—110.0
	V—145.9

FERRARI
TESTAROSSA

The Testarossa hails from a family of super autos, a family that apparently expects a great deal from the new model, having named it after one of its most revered ancestors. While each offspring eventually earns its own reputation, the Testarossa's pedigree is impeccable.

The Ferrari Testarossa has a horizontal look at first blush, but then it reveals other lines.

The new Ferrari Testarossa initially seems far removed from its namesake of almost 30 years ago. Certainly the intervening years have made their mark on the world of automobiles. Yet today's Testarossa and its heralded ancestor hail from the same family, having evolved from the imaginations of people trying to meet similar objectives. While the patriarch was conceived to be the best in racing and its namesake on par as a touring machine, they were both born of contemporary state-of-the-art technology applied to every aspect of their design and construction. Ferrari has been extremely consistent through the years.

Today's Testarossa has styling that blatantly demands attention. Its specifications incite excitement. Its pedigree is, of course, impeccable. Photographs of the car from different angles seem to distort the emphasis of the car's character in many different ways. The lines congeal when viewed in person, the

Testarossa being one of those objects that proves enigmatic to a camera's lens. Examining the Testarossa in concrete form focuses the multifaceted visual input, leaving an extremely strong impression. The first word that comes to mind to describe that impression is *horizontal*. The low and wide body lines are emphasized by the five slats that run along the sides from the front of the doors into the air intake scoops located immediately before the rear wheels—all for the sake of aerodynamics and efficient engine cooling. The lines established by the slats are echoed in the front and rear—across the nose, from taillight to taillight, between the tailpipes, and across the rear deck. Other shapes give form to the car, too, with the front being somewhat familiar in design, but with the rear flanks being reminiscent of Formula 1 or Indy car side pods. The lines that eventually give definition to the side and rear begin at the upper part of the front bumper.

Along with the outside rearview mirror, these shapes have a sensuousness about them.

The sensuousness extends into the interior, with its leather upholstery and complementary carpeting. The dash holds the speedometer and tachometer, along with oil pressure and water temperature gauges. Other gauges are placed in the vertical portion of the center console. The horizontal part of the console houses the control switches and the gated five-speed shift lever. Specially fitted luggage, embossed with Ferrari's prancing horse emblem, slides into the space behind the two seats. These pieces of luggage match the ones that fit neatly into the nose of the car. So much for luggage space.

The *really* interesting part of the Testarossa rests at the other end of the car, in the engine compartment. Ferrari's engines sound exotic, both in their descriptions and when running. First of all, the one in the Testarossa has

12 cylinders—at least four more than "normal" automobiles, eight more than most that are routinely driven for transportation. The engine is cradled in a section of the frame that detaches so that the entire power unit can be removed at once. At just under 302 cubic inches, the mechanically fuel-injected, double-overhead-camshaft powerplant turns out 390 brake horse-power—all of it powering a 3320-pound car. That's 8.5 pounds of car per horse-

Opposite page: The interior of the Testarossa has leather upholstery, gated five-speed, and gauges. Above: The horizontally opposed dohc 12-cylinder engine develops 390 bhp. It's mechanically fuel-injected. Right: One of the more predominant styling features is the use of parallel slats on either side of the car.

power, 1.29 horsepower per cubic inch —wonderful ratios for our time. In addition, Ferrari claims that the Testarossa has 0-60 times of 5.8 seconds and does a standing quarter-mile in 13.6 seconds, and that it can go almost 24 miles on a gallon of gas at a constant 55 miles per hour.

Performance of super auto quality is more than horsepower and quarter-mile times, of course. With a suspension born of racing experience, the prerequisite V-rated Goodyears or Michelins, four-wheel disc brakes, limited-slip differential built into the transmission, and rack-and-pinion steering, the Testarossa promises motoring equaled by that of few others. It's a redhead that is a credit to the family name, upholding a strong family tradition.

The 44½-inch-high Testarossa performs very well and delivers significant gas mileage for a super auto. The mid-engine layout makes some of its design elements necessary, while also contributing to its handling.

MAJOR SPECIFICATIONS

1985 Ferrari Testarossa

General: Mid-engine, rear-drive, two-seat coupe. Tubular steel chassis in two bolted parts; aluminum and steel body. **Base price:** $87,000. Ferrari S.p.a., Modena, Italy.

Dimensions and Capacities

Wheelbase (in.):	100.4
Overall length (in.):	176.6
Overall width (in.):	77.8
Overall height (in.):	44.5
Track front (in.):	59.8
Track rear (in.):	65.4
Curb weight (lbs.):	3320
Fuel tank (gal.):	30.4

Drivetrain

Engine type:
Horizontally opposed dohc 12-cylinder, four valves per cylinder

Displacement (cc/ci):	4942/301.6
Compression ratio:	9.2:1

Fuel delivery:
Twin Bosch KE Jetronic mechanical fuel injection

Net bhp @ rpm (DIN):	390 @ 6300
Net lbs/ft torque @ rpm (DIN):	362 @ 4500
Transmission type:	Five-speed manual
Final drive ratio:	3.214:1

Chassis

Front suspension:
Transverse arms, helical coil springs, hydraulic shocks

Rear suspension:
Transverse arms, two helical coil springs and hydraulic shocks per wheel, anti-roll bar

Steering:	Rack-and-pinion
Turns lock-to-lock:	3.45
Turn diameter (ft.):	39.4
Brake system:	Ventilated discs

Wheels:
Cast alloy, 8″ × 16″ front, 10″ × 16″ rear

Tires:
Front—225/50VR-16 Goodyear or 240/45VR-415 TRX Michelin; rear—225/50VR-16 Goodyear or 280/45VR-415 TRX Michelin

Performance

0-60 mph (sec.):	Est. 5.8
0-¼-mi. (sec.):	13.6
mph @ ¼-mi.:	na
Speeds in gears:	na
Top speed (mph):	Est. 180.2
Highway mpg:	Est. 23.8

Top: Testarossa's extreme width is emphasized from behind via horizontal back-panel slats. Right: Cockpit is surprisingly austere for a near–$90,000 car, but very livable.

33

BUICK WILDCAT

Memories of the Wildcats from the Fifties are of show cars, and those from the Sixties are of performance Buicks. The newest Wildcat—a drivable child of the Eighties—proudly displays advanced contemporary technology.

woop-lined show cars have not been unusual over the past few years, but the majority of them seem to have originated in Europe and Japan. Now Buick Division of General Motors has presented a show car with a name that has a familiar ring to it—Wildcat. For some, that name conjures up visions of giant red convertibles that turned heads with their power and looks in the late Sixties. Others best remember the Wildcat show cars from the Fifties.

The newest Wildcat is a drivable child of the Eighties, proudly employing some of the most advanced contemporary technology. With the Wildcat's genesis being an assignment made by Buick's performance group, the car took form in Buick Design Studio Number One. The head of that studio, William L. Porter, along with his senior designer, David P. Rand, were interviewed by Chris Poole, editor-in-chief of *Superauto Illustrated*™, and

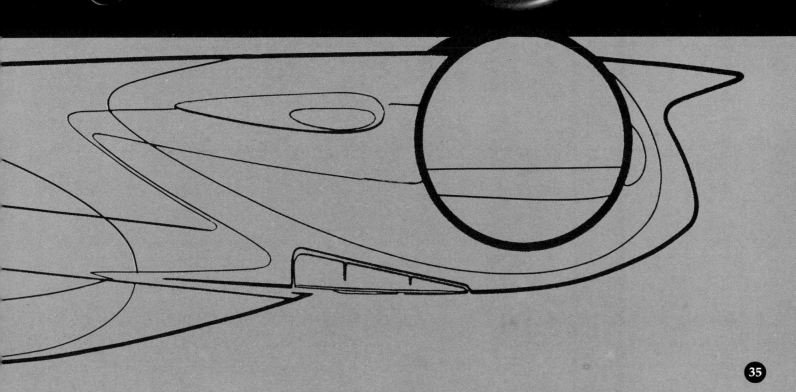

Mitch Frumkin, research and development director for the magazine, concerning where the Wildcat came from and why.

Superauto Illustrated™: What is basically the impetus for the Wildcat—how [did] you [go] about conceiving it, realizing it, and what's it all about from the design standpoint? Where's it taking you and the company?

Bill Porter: Those are pretty profound questions. Well, the original idea came from Buick's performance car specialists. That group was looking for a vehicle—in both senses of the word—to promote, to showcase, you might say, their engine development. The policy that the division had adopted some time earlier was [to pursue] very active participation in racing, as I'm sure you know. And with that general notion in mind, they apparently came to Chuck Jordan [head of General Motors Design Staff] some time ago—this would be, what, two or three years ago—it's been quite a while. And Chuck mulled it over and felt that this development on Buick's part was such a radical new thing for Buick and represented such a significant step that he felt—I believe I can speak for him to this extent—that this shouldn't really be taken lightly at all, but should be made a very serious project. Rather than just finding a designer or two and looking at a show car, he really gave it a great deal of thought and felt that it needed to be examined carefully and maybe for some time, by more than just one group. Are you aware that our services to Buick, who is, of course, our client, are structured along the lines of three separate studios? We have Buick One Studio—which is my studio—which traditionally does the intermediates and big-car exteriors.

SI: So you're the director of Buick One.

BP: Right.

SI: And where are you in the organization?

BP: Dave [Rand] is the senior designer in my studio.

SI: Okay.

BP: And then we have Buick Two Studio. In general, we do the intermediates up to the higher-priced cars, and they do the smaller cars up to the intermediates—[Buick One Studio

and] Buick Two Studio, the exterior studios. And then we have a third studio, which services all interiors—big or little, expensive or less so. At any rate, I understand that Buick Two Studio looked at this whole project and mulled it over for quite some time and had some thoughts on the subject. And then Chuck hit upon the idea—I'm not sure of the sequence of events here—he hit upon the idea of having a student design project at Center for Creative Studies downtown. Are you familiar with the leading design schools in the country?

SI: Familiar with Art Center in California.

BP: Okay. Well, the other, you might say, leading school in the country that offers a transportation design specialty is the Center for Creative Studies here in Detroit. This school has in the last decade become a definite leading con-

tender in supplying automobile designers on a worldwide basis. They are certainly on a par with Art Center School. At any rate, Chuck thought, perhaps in conversation with someone down there—I'm not too sure—the idea came up of introducing this design project to a group of seniors. Wasn't it seniors?

Dave Rand: Well, the people we had in the studio weren't seniors.

BP: No, that's right. So it must have been the junior class. It must have been a junior class assignment. That's right, because the two students came out for the summer, and they went back to complete the senior year. So it must have been the junior class in the transportation design area that was given this project. And there were 14 or 16 students in this group. And they worked on it for an entire year. They first worked on the general packaging

and arrangements. And at this point the project was given to them in such a way that they were free to try various kinds of passenger and engine configurations. I mean, it could have been

Opposite page, top: The Wildcat's front shields are the only indication that it's a Buick. Bottom: Dave Rand (left) and Bill Porter (right) were responsible for Wildcat design. Top: Canopy lifts for entrance and exit. Above: One of Dave Rand's sketches.

front engine, rear engine, anything just to see what kinds of ideas would emerge. But the fundamental notion that this was to be a car with a very strong mechanical character, and a very strong expression of mechanical themes, was one of the givens. I do know that. Bill [Robinson] and his students just really gave this a college try. I went down several times, was kind of a consultant. In fact, we had several brainstorming sessions with the students. And we even sent some engineering people down [whom] we felt would be very helpful in human factors, package layout, and so on—have them work with the students. It became a real involved project. That was a lot of fun. Finally, at some point in the semester we had hundreds of sketches, and everybody involved. The group was divided into half. Half of the students took on the interior, and half the exterior. And they were paired up, so that compatible interior and exterior people could work together. It worked out [to be] quite interesting, and led to some dramatic and ultimately, perhaps, very fruitful proposals. Then at the end of that year, two of the students were invited back to spend the summer here in my studio.

And the project was going to be continued there. No one design direction was specifically selected as a result of this student involvement. But I think it had become kind of clear by then—wouldn't you say, Dave—that it was tending toward mid-engine. At least two-thirds of the student proposals were mid-engine proposals.

DR: From what I remember....

BP: I think that had pretty much emerged: Mid-engine, four-wheel drive was the way that the project was going to go. I don't think that anybody ruled out any other possibilities at that

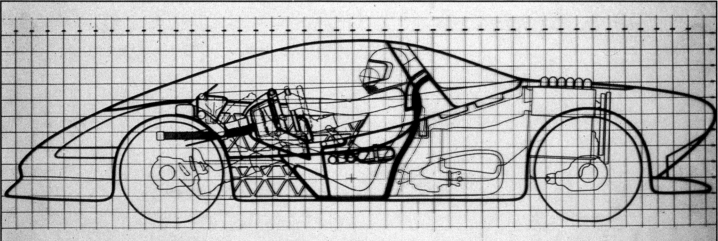

point, but I think that I certainly felt pretty clear that was far and away the dominant direction.

DR: Four-wheel drive was stated from the start.

BP: That's right. That was a given. Good point, Dave, I had forgotten. [Buick performance car people were] part of this presentation of the original problem to the students. In other words, it was not just a unilateral thing that Chuck did or I did or we did here.

DR: In fact, some of the engineering people who talked to the students were from Buick division.

SI: I would assume [Buick] also dictated the choice of powerplant.

BP: Oh yeah. Absolutely. That was a given.

SI: That and four-wheel drive.

BP: In fact, I think they even sent up mock-ups and drawings.

DR: We knew it was going to be a V-6.

BP: [And] there were discussions about whether it should be turbocharged. You know, all that, before the student involvement. At any rate, as the summer ended and closed, we had tried to sort out the general directions. And the

project was then moved out here. Since I had been so much involved in it with the students, Chuck felt it would be appropriate for it to continue in my studio. And it did. And so two students came out, and we pushed our desks around in the studio and found them a place. To my knowledge, at least in GM's history, summer students have normally not been in production automobile studios. It was kind of a first for us. Our security policy and other considerations like that to our clients tended to dictate that temporary employees are simply not privy to that information. And so this was a rare

Opposite page, top: Various sketches and color renderings were done by Buick's design staff before they settled on one direction. Bottom: Once a particular direction for the Wildcat's design was chosen, sketches made way for more accurate drawings. Note that four-wheel drive is part of the design. Left: Clay models were built, with designer Dave Rand and modeler Steve Jordan involved. Below: Although some of the details changed as the car took its final full-scale form, the Wildcat looks much like it did in the design studio.

exception. But we had the blessing of the division on that. And it's really kind of their call. So at any rate, they were there during the summer, and somehow or other at some point in the middle of the summer, all of us got into it. Even I got into it. It was like a contagious thing. And we all started developing sketches and little scale models on it. But to make a long story short, and I can't even remember all the ins and outs, one day Dave was sketching around on this project—or maybe you had been sketching for a little while—and he hit on a theme that just somehow, I don't know, it just...you know, that was in the air. Something was in the air. Dave just hit a theme that I liked instantly, and that I thought had some strange new music that was just right. And Chuck came in or maybe I went and got Chuck. I think I may have done that. Chuck came in and said, "Oh, yeah. Wow. That's it." So, you know, you turn a corner and there it is.

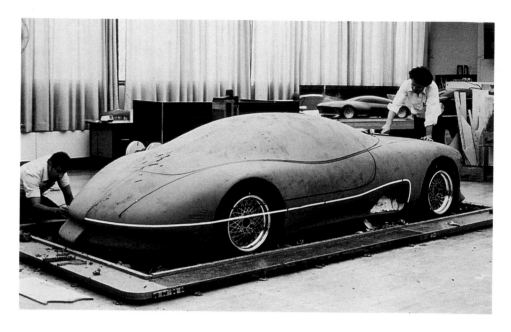

SI: Flash of inspiration.

BP: Yeah, right. Maybe it's serendipity. Whatever.

SI: Was that some of these sketches here?

DR: This is the full-size. This is what people reacted to. It was never really

one sketch that was done as the full-size. The full-size was a combination of really these two sketches. Bits and pieces...

BP: Yeah, we just kind of realized that here was a vein that we'd hit and that this felt right.

DR: This, the full-size, was what Bill and Chuck were reacting to.

BP: So then Dave roughed it up and drew a full-size version.

SI: Now you have this red version here with what looks like a huge door window.

BP: Okay, now that's somebody else's.... That was also done in that same frame.

SI: I'm fascinated by the process here.... What, if any, part did working with the students play in your creative process?

BP: Well, you know, it's probably hard

to sort that out. Most of us—well, all of us—had seen the student work, so we were familiar with the various dimensions they had explored and some of the forms they had tried.

SI: Was it interesting to you as professionals?

BP: Oh, of course. It was tremendous—rich and interesting. They had tried a lot of things. Directions they had mined, veins they had mined. Some, of course, obviously, much more successful than others. That's the way that works. I think that I felt strongly that somehow this final synthesis came out of Dave's sketches. That's just somehow what made it all click. And just what ingredients Dave's subconscious mind—let's psychoanalyze Dave—just what ingredients from the student's work went into that would be very difficult to him to say. If any.

SI: Well, again, it strikes me as a very different way for a design staff to operate. Especially from the world's largest automaker.

DR: These were very unusual circumstances. It was a very strange circumstance for me also because I had just come into the studio. So when the summer students came in, I think I came in a week after they did. And expecting to do large Buicks and instead getting this project was a surprise.

BP: Maybe that had something to do with it. I don't know. So Dave, your input from the summer students actually might have been less than [for]

someone who had been around them more. Certainly less than mine, because I actually visited the project when it was going on the previous winter. I was down there every three or four weeks at least, maybe even every two weeks. And had a lot of long, involved conversations with the students, where they would explain various points of view they [were] interested in, [with] feedback from me, and then feedback from them.

SI: That's wonderful. A real Socratic process, as it were.

BP: Well, I think so. The thing finally came together when Dave finally just hit this—whatever it was--it seemed right. I guess I felt like we had been

through a lot, that I recognized something that really had a lasting quality to it.

DR: I had only seen the student's work in the studio. I hadn't seen what CCS did over there.

BP: You had not actually been down there—no, that's right. The next step after that, then, of course, was moving

Opposite page, top: A full-scale clay model of the Wildcat was made. Bottom: "This is what it's going to look like!"—the Buick PPG Wildcat show car. Top: The Wildcat is fully operable, with one of its purposes being to showcase Buick's V-6 engine development. Above: Interior design includes a heads-up speedometer display.

this very quickly into some three-dimensional form. So from the sketches and the tape drawings, we developed a scale model of Dave's design. And Dave and—who was your modeler on that?

DR: It was Steve Jordan.

BP: Steve Jordan—a very talented guy. The forms that Steve was involved with were complex, as I'm sure you realize.

DR: There was a philosophy with the scale model and the rendering, and that was a pod pushing a pod.

SI: A pod pushing a pod?

DR: A pod for the driver, and a pod for the engine compartment. And they were kind of molded together. That was the underlying theme.

BP: They kind of interlocked or fused, sort of. The scale model, I think, expressed that.

DR: This sketch really kind of shows that.

SI: It's a very organic-form shape, very

futuristic. Now obviously General Motors never does anything without a reason. Is there something about this that suggests to you future production cars? How realistic is this to contemplate as a general styling direction for passenger cars of tomorrow?

BP: Actually, this particular car did influence a future passenger car.

DR: As to will future cars look like this, that's a question that's been asked. The project was a show car from the start. And we went at it as a show car,

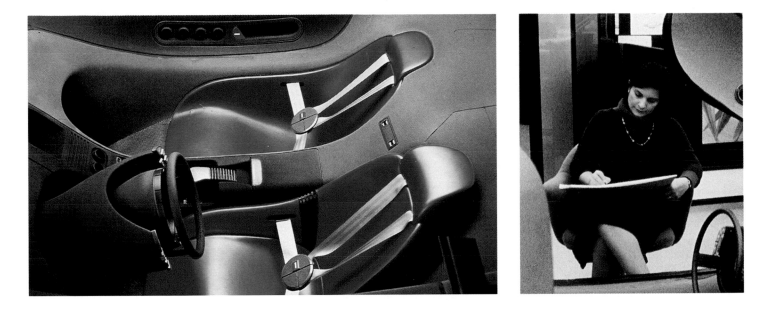

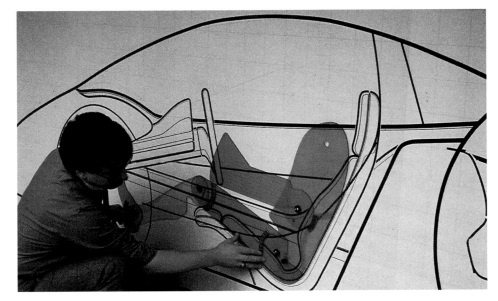

not thinking, "How will this affect other cars?"

SI: We seem to be getting back now toward the period where show cars are really idea cars, the way they were in the Fifties—where they're used not just as image-building things but as real testbeds for ideas. What are some of the ideas you think are particularly unusual about this car, and how do you think the public is going to respond to them, especially since it's being called a Buick? I mean, it could have been almost any name, but it's a very radical car for a Buick.

DR: Physically, I think the proportions are pretty radical. A number of people are kind of surprised. There was a comment at the introduction [in Las Vegas]—someone said it looked like it would go better backwards than it would forwards. I think that there was an attempt to shake up proportions and shake up what is known. Of course, we weren't responsible for the interior, but the interior was very radical also. Very new.

SI: [Who is] the woman who was handling [the interior]?

BP: Her name is Nellie Toledo—dynamite name and a dynamite lady. I think Nellie's interior is absolutely stunning, and the sculptural character of the interior is, in my opinion—I suppose words like *breakthrough* and all that are a bit trite—but it certainly represents an approach to interior form in a sculptural way that I think sets a direction for us. It wouldn't surprise me

at all if that had a fairly profound influence on our products—on our Buick products—in the coming decade or so. Without being able to pinpoint any specific arrangement or any specific feature, the overall sculptural character of the interior, I think, represents a new wave, stylistically, just as the exterior of the car did. As Dave said, this approach, this particular kind of form vocabulary, has definitely and will, I'm sure, continue to influence our products on into the Nineties. It is influencing them right now. What we're doing in the studio is being influenced by this vocabulary of forms.

DR: It's nice to know that the significance of this show car was beyond being just a show car.

SI: What do you think this says about Buick now? What sort of design statement or image statement about the Buick name were you trying to make with this? This is radical. This is really different—it's a departure; it's futuristic.

BP: Well, I think there's a very conscious attempt on all our parts to ex-

Opposite page, top: The steering wheel hub carries an electronic tachometer and other instrumentation. Center console displays less critical information, such as the G forces at work on the car. Bottom: The entire interior has a sculptured look, designed as radically as the exterior. Top left: Safety elements include four-point seat belts. Top right: The interior designers included Nellie Toledo. Above: Driver positioning was given careful consideration.

press the fact that there is definitely a change in [Buick tradition]. Buick has traditionally been, of course, a bastion of design conservatism. That's been its role for many years. In certain product areas, particularly, most of us identify the name *Buick* with pretty pricey automobiles—certainly upper middle price range on into the higher price ranges. And [they're] very conservative automobile[s]. That image, of course, is changing. And we feel that this car represents an ingredient of change in Buick's image that we would hope would be expressed dramatically and effectively. That's what we want to do.

DR: It's obvious that it's a performance car. It's an aggressive car. I think Buick would like a little more than that in their image.

SI: Looks almost like it could go right on the track.

BP: Other products in the Buick line, you know, have been showing up. I think that there are plenty of clues. If you watched Buick's lineup carefully over the last few years, you'd see plenty of clues of things moving in this direction. We just felt that this car should sum those up and express them in a very fresh and new way.

SI: You went to the wind tunnel with this car, because I think one of the shots shows the scale model—it looks like a scale model...

BP: I didn't quite finish our story of the development of the car, and I guess I should. The car's design was completed in our studio by [Dave Rand] and a modeler named Steve Jordan. And at that point we—we as a studio—had contributed, I felt, significantly to the development of the car. And we had other pressing production matters at hand—a stack of cars waiting in the hall to do, you know, waiting to get in the studio for platform time. And at this point in time, it just so happened, just fortuitously for us, that one of our advanced studios, with a really great crew, had an opening and time to do it, to work on the car. So it was sent to the Advanced Two Studio, which at that time was run by a fellow named Kip Wasenko and his assistant Dave McIn-

tosh. And they really saw the car through to completion. I think while it may have been born in Buick One Studio, it was certainly raised and educated in Advanced Two Studio. And the wind tunnel work that was done on the car was done there and resulted in some fairly significant changes from Dave's original sketch, as you would expect—the placement of the radiators dictated the side inlets, and so on. [Such things] were anticipated in some of his original sketches in a very general way, but the actual configuration was considerably altered.

DR: They made it work.

SI: Was the thought always to make it a drivable car, from the beginning?

BP: Absolutely. Absolutely. In the process of taking the basic design direction and developing it into a running and workable machine, why Kip and Dave naturally made numerous changes. And from time to time Dave and I dropped down just to see it. But at that time it really was their car. Too many cooks can spoil the stew, or whatever that old saying is...is it broth?... At

that point, Dave and I just became sort of interested bystanders and not really participants, which is appropriate, I think. So they really took the project on through to completion. And that, I think, really winds up the story.

SI: I assume that there will be some evaluation of this car as it's shown.

BP: Well, this [project] is done, you know, in conjunction with PPG, who all along intended it to be a running car and, of course, its paints and finishes and plastic materials of one sort or another are also showcased. We didn't mention that in passing, but it certainly should be because [of] their help and cooperation and sponsorship.

SI: How do you think it'll go over?

DR: If the introduction was any sort of test, I think it's going to go over very well. I think people are going to be excited about it.

SI: Who chose the name? Who chose to revive the name *Wildcat*?

BP: The name began to stick. People began to call it *Wildcat* pretty early. It dates back. I think at one point very, very early in this project it was called *Questor II*, and nobody liked that name. They felt that this was a name that had an electronic emphasis. And so we felt that, no, that was not what we were after here. And I remember us steering away from that name very consciously. But just when the name *Wildcat* hung on—it was early. We were all kind of starting to call it the *Wildcat* pretty early.

SI: Well, it identifies with the public as being Buick.

BP: And not only that, but somehow the performance aspect is intrinsic in that name. The name seems so much better.

The newest Buick Wildcat defies description. It has elements of a shark, a rocketship, a mushroom, a teardrop, and other aerodynamic-looking objects. But it's not exactly like any single one of them. The Wildcat looks slippery, certainly, but not in the manner of its contemporaries. Somehow it seems rounder, without the sharper edges of other concept cars of today.

With the design imperative being to make the car mechanical, the engine, mounted in the rear pod pushing the passenger pod, protrudes from an opening in the rear deck. In studying all of the visual input, the Wildcat appears to have the smoothness and flowing lines of a shark—and the teeth besides. One difference is that the Wildcat's teeth appear amidships rather than in the front.

The engine is a V-6, something with which Buick engineers have no small amount of experience. One only has to look at the V-6's application to recent racing efforts. Since the purpose of the Wildcat is to showcase the Buick high-performance engine and its mechanicals, the engine's features are important to note. For the one-of-a-kind show-

Opposite page: Wind tunnel testing gave designers and engineers an indication of the Wildcat's aerodynamic effectiveness. Above: From the wind tunnel information, the Wildcat's body shape and the placement of certain scoops were altered to take the greatest advantage of airflow for stability and for cooling.

and-go car, the V-6 of 231 cubic inches develops 230 brake horsepower at 6000 rpm. Dual overhead cams, four-valve heads, and Sequential-port Fuel Injection (SFI) contribute to that power output. The SFI system can be adjusted from the cockpit for varying conditions that may demand more or less performance. Another feature is Buick's Computer Controlled Coil Ignition system, replacing the more traditional coil and distributor arrangement. The Wildcat's computer analyzes variables that affect spark, contributing to the car's efficiency and performance. In addition, the engine has direct-acting hydraulic lifters, a wet sump oiling system, an oil cooler, and an electrically operated fuel pump. The engine mounts to the car ahead of the rear axle, longitudinally.

Torque feeds through General Motors' THM700-R4 four-speed automatic transmission, shifted manually, to all four wheels through a chain-driven transfer case and torque divider. Though the gears are manually shifted,

the onboard computer prevents the driver from over-revving the engine by shifting the transmission at the wrong points. The computer also shifts the transmission to first gear at a stop. The torque division is about one third to the front and two thirds to the rear—34/66 percent—for what Buick considers best for traction and handling. Handling orientation extends to the choice of wheels, tires, and braking equipment for the Wildcat. For the speeds possible from a 230-bhp 2900-pound performance automobile, a computer-controlled anti-lock brake system was deemed the best means for stopping without locking the wheels. Tires are 16-inch Goodyear V-rated Gatorbacks—225/50VR-16 front and 255/50VR-16 rear, mounted on aluminum alloy wheels.

Entering the Wildcat for a drive involves pushing a solenoid in the left rocker panel. The entire canopy of cast gray acrylic and carbon fiber with glass-reinforced polyester resin raises up at once, tilting the steering wheel

for convenient entry. While the sculptured interior is striking, the driver's information center really captures the imagination. In the center of the steering wheel, the primary instrumentation is displayed on the stationary hub. The driver monitors engine speed, ground speed, oil pressure, battery charge, fuel level, and coolant temperature via electronic instruments. In an even more futuristic manner, speed and gear selection are projected onto a panel in the driver's line of sight—a "heads-up" manner of gaining that information without taking the eyes from the road. Further, on the center console, a vacuum-fluorescent tube displays other interesting information: G forces to the front, rear, and side; horsepower; torque; spark function for tuning the engine; percent of tire slippage, by wheel; low tire pressure warning; electronic compass; and oil temperature. Note the performance orientation of most of the information, in keeping with the orientation of the automobile. Further, some controls are mounted on

pods to the left and the right of the steering wheel, with others located on the center console.

The Wildcat will be placed in the public eye at automobile shows and at PPG/CART Indy car events. General Motors design chief Chuck Jordan sums up the show car: "The Wildcat is a focal point for our latest thinking. Not only is the engineering state-of-the-art, but the styling sets a new design direction. The Wildcat represents total cooperation between design and engineering. It is a clear statement and an exciting automobile."

Opposite page: The engine compartment is exposed, showcasing the Wildcat's V-6 engine, with its four valves per cylinder and Computer Controlled Coil Ignition system. The engine is mounted ahead of the rear axle longitudinally. Below: The new Buick Wildcat takes advantage of recent technology in body composition, engine development, and chassis and drivetrain componentry. Above, right: The interior also employs recent technology, and forges on with its own.

MAJOR SPECIFICATIONS
Buick Wildcat

General: Longitudinally mounted mid-engine, four-wheel-drive, two-seat, canopy-covered concept car. Composite carbon fiber and glass-reinforced structure, front and rear steel cross members. Buick Division, General Motors Corporation.

Dimensions and Capacities

Wheelbase (in.):	102.0
Overall length (in.):	172.8
Overall width (in.):	72.3
Overall height (in.):	43.7
Curb weight (lbs):	2910
Fuel tank (gal):	15.0

Drivetrain

Engine type:
    V-6, dohc, four valves per cylinder

Displacement (cc/ci):	3800/231
Compression ratio:	9.0:1

Fuel delivery:
    Heavy-duty Sequential-port Fuel Injection

Net bhp @ rpm:	230 @ 6000
Net lbs/ft torque @ rpm:	245 @ 4000

Transmission type:
    General Motors THM700-R4 four-speed automatic

Final drive ratios: 2.14:1 front, 4.10:1 rear

Chassis

Brake system:
    Four-wheel discs, with anti-lock system

Wheels:
    Aluminum alloy, 16″ × 8″ front, 16″ × 9″ rear

Tires:
    Goodyear NCT, 225/50VR-16 front, 255/50VR-16 rear

Performance

Drag coefficient (Cd):	0.28

The Buick Wildcats: A History

The name *Wildcat* is not a new one for Buick. In the mid-Fifties, the name was used on three "dream cars" that were seen by millions of people at the General Motors Motoramas. Apparently the name had some lasting power with Buick officials, because it was resurrected in 1962 for use on the mid-priced large-body Buicks. The name continued through 1970, with slightly over a half million Buicks finally wearing the *Wildcat* badge.

The first Wildcat, now referred to as Wildcat I, bowed in 1953. According to Buick, it was built for experimental purposes only, in part to assess the feasibility of using reinforced fiberglass in production cars. The Wildcat stood only 54 inches high and sat on a 114-inch wheelbase. Power was provided by a 322-cubic-inch V-8 rated at 188 brake horsepower, coupled to Buick's Twin Turbine transmission. Pale green graced the exterior of the Wildcat I, while the interior was done up in brilliant green leather with one-inch vertical pleats. The side panels of the seats featured an insert of fine grooved chrome. The windows, top, and seat were all powered hydraulically. A special panel was designed to cover the top, and thereby eliminate the boot. "Roto-static" wheel discs were one of the more novel features of the Wildcat I, in that they remained stationary while the wheels revolved around them. Two air inlets flanked the hood ornament, providing underhood cooling for better performance. The famous Buick portholes were present, of course, but in this case they were mounted on top of the fenders. The headlight treatment was very similar to what Buick had already adopted for the 1953 production cars, except for the *V* under the parking lights. The grille bore a striking resemblance to what Buick would use on the 1954 and 1955 models.

Introduced in 1954, the Wildcat II was the sports car of the Wildcat trio, and it was the most radically styled. Described by its designers as "the only sports car with truly American styling," the Wildcat II, from the windshield back, bore a striking resemblance to the early Corvettes. Powered by the 322-cid V-8, the Wildcat II sported four carburetors to boost the horsepower to 220 bhp, transmitted through a floor-mounted Twin Turbine. As before, the body was fiberglass, this time on a 100-inch wheelbase with an overall length of 170.9 inches

and a height of 48.5 inches with the top raised. Dark tan highlighted the exterior, while the interior was finished in harmonizing two-tone tan leather. The front end of the Wildcat II generated the most interest. Buick described the fenders as being of a "flying wing" type, flaring straight out from the body and exposing the entire front wheel and part of the front suspension. The leading edge of the fender swept back over the wheel, sloping down to the lower edge of the body, thereby leaving the underside of the fender exposed. The exposed portion, along with the visible parts of the suspension, were all chromeplated. The headlights were cowl-mounted, while smaller parking/driving lights nestled under the open fender cavity. Portholes—three per side—graced the hood. The dashboard looked similar to those of production cars of the period in many respects. The Wildcat II is the only one of the three Wildcat show cars still extant. Its current home is the Al-

fred P. Sloan, Jr., Museum in Flint, Michigan. Curiously, the cowl headlights were moved into the openings under the front fenders sometime along the way, and the Wildcat hood ornament was removed.

The Wildcat III, which starred in 1955, looked more like a production car than either of its predecessors. It was a four-passenger convertible on a 110-inch wheelbase and was 190.5 inches long. As with the earlier cars, the body was made of reinforced fiberglass. The familiar V-8 again sported four carburetors, but the horsepower climbed to 280. The Twin Turbine was chosen for the transmission. Kimberly Red adorned the exterior while the interior was covered in Sovereign Red leather. The bucket seats swiveled and were separated by a floor-mounted shift lever. While the windshield was of a familiar panoramic type, the posts were vertical. Teardrop-shaped wheel cutouts dominated the side views of the car, exposing a part of the fenders'

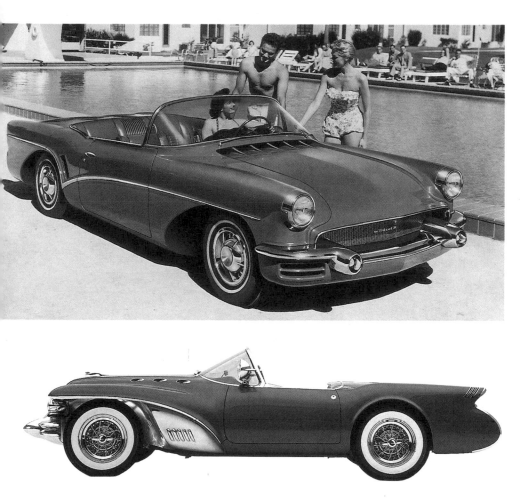

as those of the LeSabre, and they rode the same wheelbase, but the Wildcat had unique side trim and an exclusive grille treatment. A four-door sedan was added to the lineup in 1964, and a larger optional engine became available—a 425-cid V-8 with 340 bhp.

In 1965, the Wildcat grew, now sharing the Electra's 126-inch wheelbase and chassis. The series also diversified, offering the various body styles in plain, Deluxe, and Custom trims. The least expensive Wildcat was down to a $3278 sticker price, meaning that much of the previously standard equipment was now optional. Production for the year was 98,787—the all-time record high for Wildcat.

The Gran Sport performance options bowed in 1966. Included were the carry-over 401- and 425-cid engines with heavy-duty dual exhausts, heavy-duty suspension, limited-slip rear axle, and cast-aluminum rocker arm covers. A new 430-cid V-8, with 10.25:1 compression ratio and 360 bhp, was introduced for 1967. In 1968, a smaller 350-cid V-8 of 230 bhp was added, and a derivative GS350 performance package with 280 bhp was offered.

The Wildcat shrank a bit in 1969, returning to the LeSabre chassis with its 123-inch wheelbase. A new suspension, transmission, and power steering set-up were also introduced. For 1970, the last year of Wildcat production, a 455-cid 370-bhp engine became available.

Where the Wildcat left off, the Centurion picked up in 1971. It was to be the new middle-range big Buick. It would last only through 1973, however, after which Buick apparently no longer felt the need for three series of large cars. Since 1974, the LeSabre and Electra, along with the mid-size and front-wheel-drive Buicks, have filled the need.

And now Buick has a new Wildcat. Where will it lead?

undersides. Portholes were conspicuously absent. Even though the Wildcat III may have been the most conservative of the Fifties Wildcats, the grille opening and shape appeared on the 1956 Buicks. Likewise, the chrome side spear found its way onto the 1956 Roadmasters and the entire 1957 line.

After the Wildcat III had made the rounds, the name *Wildcat* gathered dust for seven years. In 1962, however, the name was revived and would be used on production line Buicks for nine years. The new Wildcat replaced the Invicta, which in 1959 had replaced the Century. Buick had first used the *Century* name in 1936. Its place in Buick's scheme of things was to serve as the division's performance car. Prewar Centurys rode on the smaller Buick bodies, but they were powered by Buick's strongest engines, gaining quite a reputation as "bankers' hot rods." The Century was revived in 1954 with a 195-bhp V-8 in the Special body. For 1959, Buick fielded a completely new line of cars. The marketing people must have felt that changing the series names would highlight the changes, and so the Invicta replaced the Century.

Then, in 1962, the *Wildcat* name was revived in the Invicta Wildcat coupe. About 2000 were made for 1962. For 1963, the *Invicta* part of the name was dropped, and the entire series became known as the Wildcat series. Nonetheless, the Wildcat continued the tradition of the Century—it was still the smaller-bodied Buick with the big engine. At least that was true at first.

The 1962 Invicta Wildcat coupe was powered by Buick's 401-cid V-8 producing 325 bhp. Wheelbase was 123 inches; overall length measured 214.1 inches; and the whole thing weighed in at 4150 pounds. The base price was $3927, and the car was well equipped at that price.

The 1963 Wildcat series consisted of two-door and four-door hardtops and a convertible. The bodies were the same

Opposite page, top: The Wildcat I show car was displayed in 1953. It featured a 322-cid V-8 that developed 188 bhp. Opposite page, bottom, and above, left: The Wildcat II of 1954 had some appearance elements in common with the Corvette, but was much more radical in its front end treatment, with the front wheel wells cut out and chromeplated. Horsepower increased to 220 bhp. Top: The Wildcat III had a hard cover protecting the lowered top. The third Wildcat was shown in 1955.

CHEVROLET CORVETTE ROADSTER

America's sports car began with that most romantic of body styles, only to lose it after 1975 due to declining sales. Now it's back, more practical than ever, and still everybody's favorite dream machine.

The newest Corvette roadster and (above) the '53 original.

In 1953, Chevrolet first brought out the Corvette—an all-American sports car. The first Corvettes were roadsters, built to be driven with the top down except in the most inclement of weather. Studying both the body and the interior styling of the car suggests that it was designed with open-air driving as its primary objective. All together, 300 fiberglass Corvettes were built in 1953, paving the way for over 800,000 more to follow over the next 32 years. Those first 300 didn't offer too many options—only a heater and an AM radio, which were built into all 300 units—and all of them were painted the same Polo white. The "Blue Flame" in-line 235.5-cubic-inch six-cylinder engine powered the car. Public response wasn't overwhelming, but Chevrolet stayed with the auto, and eventually it became a winner for the company.

As the years went by, the Corvette passed through tremendous mechanical changes, through the Stingray generation and into styling reminiscent of the Mako Shark II show car. V-8s of various sizes powered the fiberglass-body roadsters and coupes, and buyers found weights increasing by almost 800 pounds and base prices almost doubling over those of the first Corvettes by 1975. For 22 years, the roadster had made up a good portion of the make's production, with coupe models being available since 1963. From 1969 to 1975, the percentages of coupes produced were increasingly higher than those of the roadster. The 1975 model year was the last one in which Chevrolet made a Corvette convertible available, with 4629 units being produced. From then until 1986, only coupes have been offered.

The most recent generation of the Corvette was introduced for the 1984 model year. While it carried styling reflecting its 31-year heritage, leaving no doubt that it was a Corvette, the American sports car had some very high-tech engineering. The '84 was lower, shorter, and lighter than any 'Vette had been for ten years. From nose to tail, the uniframe, drivetrain, and interior showed the results of engineering and styling working closely together. The Corvettes for 1986 have been refined, maintaining the basic work introduced in 1984. According to David R. McClellan, director of Corvette engineering since 1975, the engineering keynote of the current generation's de-

sign was "form follows function." That form begins at the ground and continues throughout the car.

Although the Goodyear Eagle Gatorbacks have appeared on other vehicles since '84, they were developed specifically for the Corvette by Goodyear. The VR speed rating of the 245/50VR-16 tires refers to one of several speed ratings for tires used in Europe—VRs are designed for speeds in excess of 140 miles per hour, which are within the capabilities of the 'Vette. The Gatorback tread design is intended to shed water effectively to resist hydroplaning. The Eagles are unidirectional. So are the wheels, owing to the shape of their cooling fins. Equipped with the optional Z51 Performance Handling Package, a coupe is capable of up to .95 G lateral acceleration.

The chassis has as much to do with

the cornering ability as the tires do. For the current generation, Chevrolet abandoned its favored perimeter-type frame for a new steel-backbone design. The spine takes the form of a C-section beam that carries the propshaft and is connected rigidly to the differential, benefiting the car through less weight and more cockpit room by eliminating the transmission and differential cross members. It also allows the dual exhaust system to run under the propshaft instead of alongside it.

Welded to the frame is what Chevy calls an "integral perimeter-birdcage

Top: The first Corvette roadster, in 1953. Above: Before 1986, the last Corvette roadster, in 1975. Opposite page, top: The 1986 Corvette roadster stands before a new-generation coupe. Bottom: The '86 roadsters have ABS and VATS, two safety systems.

unitized structure''—a uniframe—making it the first Corvette to employ unitized construction instead of separate body-on-frame. The birdcage forms the windshield and door frames, lower front pillar extensions, rocker panels, rear cockpit wall, and front subframe. It also includes the hoop at the rear of the cockpit, which acts as the attachment point for the back window of the coupe. The entire structure is galvanized inside and out for corrosion resistance, and it acts as a skeleton for hanging major body panels, which are still made of fiberglass. Completing the basic assembly is an aluminized, bolt-on front bumper carrier. A similar bolt-on extension supports the back bumper.

To match the new chassis, Chevy gave the Corvette a heavily reworked suspension. The front end has unequal-length upper and lower A-arm arrangements with a fiberglass-reinforced plastic leaf spring mounted transversely between the two lower arms. An anti-roll bar is standard. In the rear, the suspension consists of a five-link setup, with upper and lower longitudinal links mounted between the hub carriers and the body, twin lateral strut rods connecting the differential with the hub carriers, another transverse plastic leaf spring, plus U-jointed half-shafts and rear-mounted tie-rods.

Stopping power comes from vented disc brakes at each wheel, hydraulically assisted. The brakes were a new design

for the '84 Corvette—they were created by Girlock, an American offshoot of the British Girling company. Making extensive use of aluminum, the brakes have 11.5-inch rotors, and they feature quick-change semimetallic pads and audible wear sensors.

The same engine that has powered all Corvettes since 1981 has returned for 1986—the 5.7-liter V-8. It utilizes the Bosch hotwire multipoint fuel injection system that Chevrolet introduced in 1985. New features on the engine for '86 include centrally located copper core spark plugs, larger inlet ports, and sintered metal valve seats. The engine may be coupled to a four-speed overdrive automatic or four-plus-three manual.

The new-generation Corvette has an interior that is as contemporary as its

chassis. The cockpit is dominated by a space-age instrument panel and the usual tall center tunnel/console. Instrumentation is directly ahead of the driver—an all-electronic display. Digital and analog displays monitor road speed and engine speed, while minor functions are monitored as numerical readouts in a smaller panel flanked by the two main displays. A switch panel in the vertical portion of the center console allows the driver to select which functions will be monitored, including such things as instantaneous and average miles per gallon, trip odometer, and fuel range, all of which are calculated by the onboard engine computer. The console also houses the sound system controls, a warning light panel, and heating/ventilation controls.

Two systems that bear mentioning for 1986 are the Vehicle Anti-Theft System (VATS) and the computerized anti-lock braking system (ABS). Both are standard equipment. VATS is electronic, with sensors in the doors and hatch that trigger the alarm. Should a thief thwart the sensors, using the wrong key will render ignition impossible. Delays of up to a half hour could be faced by a thief in attempting to start the Corvette, and that length of time is too long for most thieves to endure.

The anti-lock braking is based on the Bosch ABS II design. Computerized, the system acts to prevent the brakes from locking during panic stops, while at the same time making maximum use of the traction possible through each wheel. Sensors in each wheel determine when it is beginning to lock. The information from the sensors is monitored by the computerized control unit, which modulates the brake pressure hydraulically. The result is pulse-like

control throughout the braking procedure that prevents loss of control due to skidding. Handling is also improved, with less effort needed to correct the steering of the car.

Changes in the coupe version of the Corvette were necessary to produce Corvette convertibles with appropriately rigid bodies. Birdcage pieces have been reinforced with stronger braces and cross members, and added reinforcements were given to the uniframe. Door latches were strengthened. The top mechanism was made of aluminum

in order to reduce its mass. Besides other subtle suspension and steering differences, the convertibles all have the 9.5-inch wheels of the coupe's Z51 Performance Handling Package. The Z51 is not available in the convertible.

The 1986 Corvette roadster will be very visible this spring, because the car has been chosen to pace the Indianapolis 500. In its yellow and black markings, the pace car is essentially stock—the first stock pace car since the last time the Corvette led the championship cars around the 2½-mile oval for the

May classic in 1978. The roadster adds another dimension to the Corvette story. Some people would even argue that the roadster version is the way all Corvettes should be produced.

Opposite page, top: The roadster's uniframe modifications in white. Bottom: 350-cid engine. Top: This year's Indy pace car. Above, left: The last stock Indy pace car. Above, right: Posed by Chevrolet's monument.

	1953 The First Corvette	1975 The Last Roadster	The Latest Roadster
Base price:	.$3513	$6550	$32,480
Production (no. of units):	300	4629	na
Chassis:	Perimeter frame	Perimeter frame	Backbone-type
Body:	Fiberglass, on frame	Fiberglass, on frame	Fiberglass, uniframe
Wheelbase (in.):	102.0	98.0	96.0
Overall length (in.):	167.0	185.5	176.5
Overall width (in.):	72.2	69.0	71.0
Curb weight (lbs):	2705	3475	Est. 3150
Engine type:	ohv inline six-cylinder	ohv V-8	ohv V-8
Displacement (cc/ci):	3859/235.5	5735/350.0	5735/350.0
Compression ratio:	8.0:1	8.5:1/9.0:1	9.0:1/9.5:1*
Bhp @ rpm:	150 @ 4200 (SAE gross)	165 @ 3800/205 @ 4800 (SAE net)	230 @ 4000 (SAE net)
Fuel delivery:	Carburetors	Carburetors	Multipoint fuel injection

*With aluminum cylinder heads

Driving Impression:
Chevrolet Corvette Roadster

Maxims for our time:
- Real motorcycles are black.
- Never try to eat anything bigger than your head.
- Check oil level and tire pressure once a week.
- Be prepared.
- Blowing your nose incorrectly will hurt your ears.
- Don't panic.
- Honest sports cars have convertible tops.

For the first time since 1975, Chevrolet has made its Corvette an honest sports car. The roadster is an option. Open-top driving, fresh air, freedom—convertibles are as close as you can come to riding a motorcycle and feeling as if you're a part of the surroundings. After more than a decade's absence, the ragtop's reintroduction brought with it a certain amount of apprehension. The Corvette of 10 years ago was almost like a creature from another place and time. How would the new roadster withstand the transition to the Corvette's new body style?

The scene was Yosemite National Park in late summer/early Indian summer—the weather was gorgeous, with record heat being recorded in surrounding parts of California. Accepting an invitation to drive the new Corvette roadsters had been a matter of course,

something about which little time for thought was allowed. Hop a plane to Fresno, journey north to just short of the park, and be prepared to drive. Yanking someone from behind a desk in the Midwest and expecting him to cope with California mountains behind the wheel of a Corvette roadster has to be somewhat akin to the radical changes faced by a baby first encountering the harsh realities beyond the womb.

Mountains present almost any automobile with breathing problems, let alone the driver. While sunrise in the mountains is clean, crisp, and bright, inviting hearty appetites and prompting the need for sunglasses, thin mountain

air also promises to sap the strength of any red-blooded nonturbocharged automobile, even a blustery Corvette. As two groups of the make lined up in front of the temporary quarters, awaiting their drivers and passengers, the dread of engine wheeze struck home. Sustaining performance would be difficult. The tops were lowered, with only the side windows raised. That didn't last long, either—if the top's going to be lowered, so should the windows. Another maxim?

The design of the recent-generation Corvette coupe is fairly clean, but the roadster version of the 'Vette's body is slick. Take off the lump of a roof from

behind the windshield, cover the space behind the seats with a flat fiberglass piece that blends into the rear deck (and covers the folded top), and the automobile embodies the word *roadster*. Six of the Chevy ragtops stood in a row, all of them begging to be taken onto the road.

Opening the top of the Corvette distracts almost anyone's attention from the interior, whether the seating or instrumentation. They don't force themselves on you, providing a comfortable, supportive driving position that you can adjust quickly and an electronic dashboard that is one of the most visible displays in daylight among all of the

electronic dashes available at this time. Controls for the mirrors and seats are at hand, and once their locations are memorized, they are easily operated by touch. The body-mounted shift lever is a quick motion of the right hand away from the steering wheel. Shifts have a mechanical feel—not liquid or fluid like a Volvo, but not as vague as some of the cable-actuated linkages either.

Opposite page: Other than slanting more to minimize the sun's glare, the dashboard hasn't changed much from the 1984's. Above: Wide rubber, a strong engine, and an open top make the roadsters pleasurable.

The tops were lowered, with only the side windows raised. That didn't last long either.

The first group of cars to be encountered all had manual transmissions. Nothing wheezy could be attributed to the performance of the Corvette roadsters, although the Chevrolet engineers assured the drivers that the cars wouldn't run as well at 8000 feet as they would in the Arizona desert. So be it. Taking the first turn onto the winding mountain roads, the clutch felt substantial without needing overwhelming pressure. It wasn't as awkward to use as those in some of the more recent pony cars. Another aspect of the 'Vette that feels good is the sense of space from the cockpit to the front bumper. The rise in the fenders isn't so much that you think that you're driving a slingshot rail.

Little time was given to familiarization before reaching touring speed on the twisting and hilly terrain. But the Corvette is forgiving enough for you to jump in and go without a great deal of preparation. While on the one hand you know that enough horsepower lies underfoot, you also understand that abuse of that power will put you into dire straits. The car is forgiving and tractable enough for running around town, but it's also strong enough to get you into trouble if not respected. Describing the roadster's personality as Jekyll-and-Hyde wouldn't be fair; referring to it as a gentle giant perhaps would be better.

Something should be said about tires and wheels. Very few automobiles on the road today have adequate contact with the ground. The Gatorbacks of the Corvette give testimony to their development for the car—the package has to be pushed beyond reasonable driving limits to make the car do something unusual. Corkscrewing, turning, angling through the mountain curves never caused doubt about the ability of the 'Vette or the rubber meeting the road. Only the ability of the driver remained questionable.

Thinking of being able to "throw around" a 3100-pound automobile brings to mind some amusing images, but after a while—after encountering never-ending sequences of turns—you have the feeling that the roadster is capable of some nimble maneuverings. Still, it has the nimbleness of a tiger rather than that of a cheetah, when all is said and done. Yet that's a far cry from the more ponderous offerings of the past. The roadster's catlike feet not

only corner with assurance, holding the car's body flat in combination with its suspension, but work in conjunction with the new anti-lock braking system (ABS) to pull down the speed of the auto without its sliding. Finding a clear stretch of highway to the rear took some doing, but slamming the brake pedal as close to the floorboard as possible made the wait worthwhile. No skidding resulted from the overambitious braking maneuver, although

some slight steering corrections were necessary.

With more than adequate acceleration, tires and wheels suited to the handling needs of most drivers, and a visually and physically supportive interior, the roadster has a suspension that's taut, but certainly livable for long distances. If the luggage area were of greater capacity, the roadster would cry out to be taken for a long-distance tour. Creative packing will provide you with your necessities, with perhaps the addition of a luggage rack. However, cluttering up the rear deck would be a shame.

So pull out the small, soft-sided suitcases and pack up the most tightly foldable clothes from the closet. The time has come for some open-air fun. Put down the top, and head for the warm weather. A few thousand miles in the Corvette roadster will probably leave you yearning for even more.

Opposite page, top: 1986 Corvette roadsters were lined up in the mountain morning, waiting to be driven for a day-long test session—the ultimate temptation? Bottom: Some drivers were tempted more than others. Top: The best way to enjoy mountain air is from a roadster with the top lowered. Above, left: Complying with current legislation, the middle stoplight is mounted in the center of the rear deck. Above, right: Vent slots in the wheels determine the direction in which they're to turn. Tires were developed in parallel to the unidirectionality of the Corvette's wheels.

Once again, a new Corvette allows you to put the top down instead of taking it off, great news for open-air lovers everywhere. It's a car that beckons you to spend a few thousand miles under the sun—and it'll always leave you yearning for more.

The aggressive Pantera GT5 boldly addresses
the future, its form belying the fact that its
basic design is 15 years old.

62

DE TOMASO PANTERA GT5

More than additional bodywork maintains the Pantera as a contemporary super automobile. Vast improvements have been made on the car during the 10 years since it was last offered for sale in the United States.

The vicious-looking body has a sloping hood, pointed nose, and aggressive air dam. The short rear sweeps up from the wheel wells to meet the deck. The lid behind the driver with its two "flying buttresses" obviously covers an engine. For all of the contemporary, even futuristic styling, imagining the design to be 15 years old is hard. A discerning eye readily finds the original lines beyond the air dam, flared fenders, and rear-mounted wing. The lines are of the de Tomaso Pantera and they are as they were in 1970, lurking beneath the added bodywork of the Pantera GT5. But it's more than additional bodywork that maintains the Pantera as a contemporary super automobile. Vast improvements have been made on the Pantera during the 10 years since it was last sold in the United States.

The Pantera story began in the early Sixties, when builder and driver Alejandro de Tomaso was putting together formula cars and sports racers in Italy. De Tomaso enthusiastically followed up inspirations for advancing automotive and racing design with fitful projects that met with varying degrees of success, including "flexible" suspensions and his own engine. In 1964, the expatriate Argentine decided that it was time to build a GT car, and he produced a mid-engine vehicle that he called the Vallelunga. Powered by a 1500cc English Ford engine, the car wasn't very fast, but it was a good effort on de Tomaso's part. The Vallelunga experience led to one of de Tomaso's best achievements —the Mangusta, a beautiful automobile from every angle, an exotic GT that performed as well as it looked. A 289-cid Ford powerplant spirited the Mangusta to 155 mph. Again with a mid-engine design, de Tomaso's Mangusta also featured a German ZF five-speed transaxle, a limited-slip differential, four-wheel Girling disc brakes, air conditioning, and wheels that imitated race cars by being larger in the rear than in the front. The Mangusta sold for about $11,000 in the United States. The Mangusta and de Tomaso's race-car-building efforts were successful enough by 1970 that he could acquire two respected Italian coachbuilding firms, Ghia and Vignale. The conglomerate of designers and builders set about the task of redesigning the Mangusta to eliminate its problems of ponderous handling and inefficient space utilization, with

the result being the Pantera. Meanwhile, Ford Motor Company, familiar with de Tomaso because of supplying engines for the Mangusta and the new Pantera, bought the company and began to distribute the Pantera in the U.S.

The de Tomaso Pantera was imported by Ford-Lincoln-Mercury from 1971 to 1974, at which time the company's distribution ceased due to the company's inability to certify the car in compliance with safety and emissions regulations. The Ford Motor Company mass-marketed the Pantera, and 5269 units were sold in the three years that it was offered. The Pantera listed at a

base price of $10,000 and maintained the best elements of the Mangusta—the mid-engine layout, ZF transaxle, disc brakes, independent suspension, and unit body/chassis. Many of the Mangusta's design problems were eliminated, and a larger-displacement engine powered the Pantera. Its 351-cubic-inch Ford Cleveland V-8 developed 310 brake horsepower and was capable of an estimated 162 miles per hour. But the Pantera was plagued by a number of problems that tarnished its reputation in America. For instance, when the government first ran crash tests, the Pantera tended to explode. Ford ordered

The original lines of the Pantera (left) can readily be found on the GT5 (above), despite the added bodywork. Look beyond the air dam, flared fenders, and rear-mounted wing to find the original design. Improvements have been made on the car over the last 10 years, with refinements in the chassis, engine, interior, and body that have left very little of the last decade's super auto untouched.

MAJOR SPECIFICATIONS

De Tomaso Pantera GT5

General: Mid-engine, rear-drive, two-seat coupe. Unit steel body. **Base price:** $55,000. **Importer:** Stauffer Classics, Ltd., Blue Mounds, WI.

Dimensions and Capacities

Wheelbase (in.):	98.8
Overall length (in.):	168.1
Overall width (in.):	77.6
Overall height (in.):	43.3
Track front (in.):	59.4
Track rear (in.):	62.2
Curb weight (lbs.):	3268
Fuel tank (gal.):	21.1

Drivetrain

Engine type:	Ford ohv V-8
Displacement (cc/ci):	5763/351
Compression ratio:	8.5:1
Fuel delivery:	One Holley four-barrel
Net bhp @ rpm (SAE):	350 @ 6000
Net lbs/ft torque @ rpm (SAE):	333 @ 3800
Transmission type:	ZF five-speed manual
Final drive ratio:	2.95:1

Chassis

Front suspension:
Unequal-length A-arms, coil springs, tube shocks, anti-roll bar
Rear suspension:
Unequal-length A-arms, coil springs, tube shocks, anti-roll bar

Steering:	Rack-and-pinion
Turns lock-to-lock:	3.4
Turn diameter (ft.):	39.4

Brake system:
11.2" vented discs front, 11.1" vented discs rear, vacuum assist
Wheels:
Campagnolo cast alloy, 15" × 10" front, 15" × 13" rear
Tires:
Pirelli P7, 285/40VR-15 front, 345/35VR-15 rear

Performance

0-60 mph (sec.):	Est. 5.5
0-¼-mi. (sec.):	Est. 14.0
mph @ ¼-mi.:	99.5
Speeds in gears:	I—45
	II—69
	III—97
	IV—112
	V—137
EPA city mpg:	na
EPA highway mpg:	na

design changes. The electrical system gave some owners fits, too, as did problems with overheating, rust, wheel bearings, and U-joints. But it was the bumper regulations that halted importation of the Pantera in 1974.

Ten years later, the Pantera returns. The de Tomaso Pantera GT5 maintains the body design and essential drivetrain of the original version, and some of the suspension components have not been changed. Just about everything else has. One of the differences is in the source of the Ford 351-cid engine. Where the first Panteras used Cleveland 351s, the current models are powered by stronger four-barrel-carbureted versions of the engine as it is manufactured in Australia. There are two power options of either 300 or 350 bhp. The car is capable of 0-60 times under 6.0 seconds and a top speed of over 180 mph. In addition, the engine can be modified easily by aftermarket specialists to produce even greater horsepower, simply by employing turbocharging and other performance-oriented parts and techniques. The additional flaring of the fenders over the wheel wells houses Pirelli P7s, 285/40VR-15s front and 345/35VR-15s rear, which carry the front/rear weight distribution of

42.7%/57.3%. The performance of the car is further enhanced by oversized brakes, vented rotors, and functional scoops front and rear that direct air to the brakes. Base price of the car is now $55,000, which delivers an all-leather interior, burled wood accents surrounding full conventional instrumentation, power windows, and air conditioning as standard. Weighing 3268 pounds, the GT5 stands 43.3 inches tall on a wheelbase of 98.8 inches. The U.S. distributor, Stauffer Classics, Ltd., expects 50–70 units to be made available to the American marketplace in 1985, making Panteras rare. The limited

numbers are due to the process of building the Pantera by hand, to the point of finishing the body in hand-rubbed lacquer.

Although the Pantera has had a history colored by diverse problems, the current GT5 model promises to redeem the name. Pantera importer George Stauffer: ''I want to see it available again in the U.S. But this time as the quality automobile the de Tomaso name stands for in Europe....''

Stauffer Classics, Ltd.
10967 Division Street
Blue Mounds, Wisconsin 53517

Opposite page: Only 50-70 units of the hand-built, Ford-powered, mid-engine Pantera will be made available to the American marketplace in 1985. The angular super automobile will be quite rare. Above: Standard equipment in the interior includes leather upholstery, burled wood accents, power windows, and air conditioning. The dashboard sports full conventional instrumentation.

BEYOND DE TOMASO

The Xaver Jehle company of Switzerland is engaged in the industrial design and manufacture of light metal automobile chassis. It also produces a small series of modified automobiles, based on some of the world's super autos. Any of a number of various makes may be changed to a customer's specifications, utilizing company design elements and performance parts—Lamborghinis and de Tomaso Panteras are among those altered by Xaver Jehle.

A Pantera completely modified by the company has undercarriage and braking system improvements, both of which are redesigned to handle the additional torque caused by the engine's increased output. Horsepower of various levels is possible, depending upon the ultimate use of the automobile.

The complete package for a Pantera includes the following: large front spoiler with increased air intake, mudguard widening, oil-cooler air inlet, cooling system for the cylinder heads, carburetors with aluminum screen and filter, and a rear spoiler. All exterior vehicle parts are fitted together without seams, leaving the body looking very clean. Materials for the exterior are quality-controlled by West German technicians.

Interiors sport the best English leather, which is available in any color. Taller customers of Xaver Jehle can be fitted with specially designed seats for greater comfort. Further modifications of the Pantera include custom paint, a chromium exhaust system, aluminum oil sump with cooling ribs, performance crankshaft, electronic ignition, oil cooler, and improved valve gearing. Four-valve cylinder heads are available, as are four two-barrel Weber carburetors, wrought-iron pistons, and titanium coils.

The custom work of the Xaver Jehle company further demonstrates the timelessness of the Pantera design, and the inherent ability that the Pantera has to continue as a super auto.

Left: The pieces added to a Pantera by the Xaver Jehle company grace the body without seams. Below: Engines are available at different levels of horsepower, with many Jehle parts. Bottom: Wing and air scoops are added to fully modified Panteras. Opposite page: Interiors can be custom ordered so that tall people will be comfortable in seats modified for them.

PORSCHE 959

Rallying inspires the development of some of the world's most intriguing, most advanced road vehicles. Porsche's challenger could be called the ultimate 911. But it's much more than that, thrusting the company into the next century.

The Porsche 959 features rally technology (opposite page) with 911-like features.

Since the introduction of its Type 356 sports cars in the early Fifties, Porsche's automobiles have captured the imaginations and fancies of countless enthusiasts everywhere. Twenty years ago, the company strengthened its hold with the introduction of the new 911/912 models (the 911 had a six-cylinder engine; the 912 had a four). The 911's impact on the marketplace has been such that, despite Porsche's introduction of non-911-based models since, the 911 is the type with which Porsche seems destined to be identified well into the next century. Of course, variations on the 911's theme have been produced through the last two decades. Now another derivative stirs the boiling waters in the caldron of automotive dreams—a super auto designated the 959.

Where does something like the 959 come from, and why? What prompts the development of such esoteric equipment in such exotic automobiles? Racing, of course, is the answer—at least in Porsche's case. High visibility for any given company results from its ability to field successful competitors for the various racing events around the world. The Type 959 was developed to compete in rallying, and early prototype units have proven successful under excruciatingly cruel circumstances in Africa. In order to qualify the car to compete in Group B, 200 roadworthy units of the 959 have to be offered by Porsche. They are, and they already have designated buyers, for the most part. With all of the sophisticated electronics, hydraulics, and bodywork utilized by Porsche, the car won't be inexpensive. The super auto has a super price—somewhere around $130,000—a far cry from the near-$5000 base-model price of the first 911/912s in the mid-Sixties.

Perhaps the best description of the 959's appearance is that it obviously has been derived from the 911's styling. Window glass and the roofline are the strongest direct visual carry-overs from the established model, but other than that, Porsche's engineering is about

Below: The 959 shares only glass and shape with the 911. Upper left: The rally car has been considered successful in its initial outings. Upper right: The dual turbocharger system operates in two stages.

all that is held in common by the two types. Development was virtually from scratch. While the body looks like it's a 911 body, the proportions are different. Porsche could have shaped it in any manner they wished, but apparently desired the identification afforded by the 911-like shape. The central thrust of the aerodynamics applied to the body shape was to reduce lift as much as possible, with a low drag coefficient of importance, also. Using 1/5-scale models and then full-scale ones in wind tunnels, a body was shaped that combines aesthetic beauty with lift-free, low-drag (0.32 Cd) aerodynamics. The body is also built for strength and for light weight, employing such high-tech materials as aluminum alloys, polyurethane, and aramid-fiber compound for the skin and galvanized steel for the rigid safety-cell framework. The body is flexible where necessary, such as in the area of the polyurethane front spoiler, and rust resistant in others, such as in the frame. Along the bottom of the car, a flat pan reduces air turbu-

lence and contributes to the lack of lift on the body. All in all, the 959 looks to all the world like an Eighties and Nineties 911, with gorgeous curves, spoilers, and air dams that will carry the 911 style into the years (perhaps decades)

ahead. The drivetrain and chassis are equal to the demands of the future, too.

In the engineering of the 959's turbocharged powerplant, certain goals were foremost in the minds of the development team: The engine should be capa-

ble of good acceleration and high power output at the top end of the rpm range, as well as being as fuel-efficient as possible. Usually, turbocharging an engine gives it added muscle, but low-rpm power and its initial acceleration capabilities are relatively flat. The problem is in waiting for the turbo to kick in so that it can be effective. Small turbochargers alleviate some of the problems caused by waiting to overcome the inertia of a larger one, but the responsiveness comes at the expense of not being able to achieve maximum torque and nonefficient use of fuel. Porsche has engineered a more balanced system that has two turbochargers that work in two stages. One of the turbos is set up to receive a constant flow of exhaust gas in a more or less "normal" application of the technology, despite the Rube Goldberg type of plumbing. That plumbing initially sends all of the exhaust gases to only the one turbo. Then, in the upper engine-speed range, the plumb-

ing is electronically controlled to allow the second turbocharger to kick in and to share equally in the production of boosted air for the engine. Aiding in the efficiency of the turbocharging system, two large air-to-air intercoolers are part of the plumbing—they are situated at the engine's flanks. The 2850cc horizontally opposed six-cylinder engine develops 450 brake horsepower at 6500 rpm.

The rest of the drivetrain is just as complex. The engine couples to the transaxle via a six-speed gearbox. Half-shafts turn the rear wheels, and the transaxle continues to the front wheels. Along with the five-speed gearing is a forward gear marked G—Gelände, meaning "terrain" or "off-road." The G gear is intended for slogging through mud or snow; it's much lower than regularly would be applied to road driving. In that regard, G is not unlike the double-low that's offered in light and midsize trucks. But the most fascinating part of the drive system is not in the gearing. Rather, it's in the application of engine torque to the road through the four-wheel drive. The variable system can be fine-tuned to different road conditions, with a switch that allows the driver to match the type of drive to the road conditions: The driver can choose traction (locked), ice and snow, wet, and dry settings. In addition, wheel sensors detect slip, and

through a hydraulic system, electronics increase the contact force of the wheels where it's most needed. Evaluations take place in a continuing process. The variable four-wheel drive could distribute the torque from anywhere between a 50-percent split front and rear to all of it applied at the rear wheels.

In addition to the microprocessed torque-splitting, another system raises and lowers the suspension of the car. The leveling is in response to the different conditions encountered in rallying, including everything from off-road conditions (for which the top setting clears the ground by almost 2½ inches above its normal setting) to high-speed paved surfaces. Should the driver neglect to reduce the height when passing from rougher terrain to smoother, increasing speed correspondingly, the micros make sure that the body lowers closer to the road proportionally. Another automatically adjusted part of the car is its shock absorber system: Shock rate, too, can be varied, from soft to firm, in accordance with the type of driving that's being done. The ride becomes firmer as the speed increases, should the necessary changes in the settings be ignored by the driver.

The tires and wheels are special, also. Behind the flush wheel covers, the magnesium wheels have spokes that

are hollow, opening into the wheel rim and, consequently, the tires. Two pressure switches are built into the rims to monitor air pressure, maintaining an electronic watch system that reports loss of air pressure on a dashboard gauge. The gauge indicates exactly which tire is losing pressure. At the same time, the 235/40VR-17 front and 255/40VR-17 rear Dunlop Denloc tires mounted on the hollow-spoked wheels were designed to maintain their hold on the rims in case of a blowout, helping the driver to control the car at high speeds. The wheels and tires complement the anti-lock braking system used in the car.

The various systems operating as parts of the chassis and drivetrain plant the 959 into something like Tomorrow Land. Crossing from rough dirt road to high-speed autobahn brings into play the full range of the automatic leveling,

continued on page 80

Opposite page, top: 200 road-car versions of the 959 homologate it for rallying. Middle: The 959's rear deck. Bottom: A familiar shape that has a suspension that raises and lowers, shocks that vary in rate, and a four-wheel-drive system with ABS—all automatic. Above: Drive the 959 anywhere, and quickly!

Significant changes have been applied to the
Porsche line since the introduction of the 356s.
While the 911s have continued to ensure
Porsche's niche in automotive history, the 959s
go beyond to thrust the company into the future.

Clockwise from the engine, the cutaway reveals much of the technology brought to bear in the Porsche 959: The engine has twin overhead cams and four valves per cylinder, as well as two turbochargers and intercoolers. The six-speed transmission has a double-low gear for extreme road conditions. Four different drive configurations may be chosen for the four-wheel-drive system. Radiators in the front cool water and oil. Shocks have variable rates, and the suspension may be set at different heights. The Dunlop tires mount on hollow-spoked wheels that have air-pressure sensors. The anti-lock braking system is computer controlled.

shock settings, variable four-wheel drive, and, without doubt, shifting of stages in turbocharging from the double-turbocharged engine. The car seems to be as computerized as a spacecraft!

Interior appointments reflect their heritage, having been popped from the same mold as the 911 seats, dash, and general layout. Yet, for its familiarity, the interior is entirely new. The tachometer takes up the center part of the instrument cluster, flanked by gauges and lights on the right and left. Unique to the 959, though, are the lights for the low-air-pressure sensors, the controls for the variable drive setting, and those for the shocks and leveling on the console. The super Porsche was conceived as a long-distance traveler, as its electronically controlled environment attests. Leather trim matches the color of the exterior.

Significant changes have been applied to the Porsche line since the introduction of the 356s. While the 911s have continued to ensure Porsche's niche in automotive history, the 959s go beyond to thrust the company's reputation into the future.

The lightweight body of the Porsche 959 is made of various materials, including aramid-fiber compounds, polyurethane, and aluminum alloys.

MAJOR SPECIFICATIONS
Porsche 959

General: Rear-engine, variable four-wheel-drive, two-door coupe. **Price:** Est. $130,000. Dr. Ing. h. c. F. Porsche Aktiengesellschaft, Stuttgart, Germany.

Dimensions and Capacities

Wheelbase (in.):	90.3
Overall length (in.):	167.7
Curb weight (lbs):	Est. 2975
Fuel tank (gal):	23.8

Drivetrain

Engine type:
Horizontally opposed dohc six, four valves per cylinder, air-cooled, water-cooled cylinder heads

Displacement (cc/ci):	2850/174
Compression ratio:	8.0:1

Fuel delivery:
Individual cylinder injection, two injectors per cylinder, twin two-stage turbocharging with two air-to-air intercoolers

Net bhp @ rpm:	450 @ 6500
Transmission type:	Six-speed manual
Final drive:	4.12:1

Chassis

Front and rear suspension:
Dual transverse arms and dual shock absorbers, adjustable shock stiffness and ride level
Brake system:
Anti-lock brake system, four-piston brake calipers on ventilated disc brakes
Wheels:
Hollow-spoke magnesium, with center-lock hubs
Tires:
Dunlop Denloc, 235/40VR-17 front, 255/40VR-17 rear

Performance

Top speed (mph):	Est. 180+
0-60 mph (sec):	Est. 4.0